Praise for Economic Development Online:

"In the new world of economic development marketing, there are two options: Change or Fail. For those interested in the former, read and fully digest *Economic Development Online*. Anatalio Ubalde explains the basics of dozens of emerging tools and why they matter to today's economic developers."

—Andy Levine, President and Chief Creative Officer, Development
  Counsellors International

"Anatalio Ubalde captures readers through his clear, easy to understand explanation of what an avid economic development professional requires to be successful in today's Internet-centric world. To be effective, embrace and implement the best practices he outlines in *Economic Development Online*."

—Judy McKinney Cherry, CEcD, Principal, New Growth Strategies
  & Former Cabinet Secretary, State of Delaware Economic
  Development Office

"The competition to reach business decision makers in today's challenging economic climate is fierce. Economic development marketers must focus on strategies that will deliver results. This authoritative book delivers on all counts with tested strategies backed by real-world case studies. The book is a must read for economic development practitioners."

—Janet Fritz, Director of Marketing and Technology, Metro Denver
  Economic Development Corporation

"The Internet is an ideal place to connect businesses with customers. This book ingeniously shows how to connect economic developers with businesses."

—Miriam Warren, Vice President of European Marketing, Yelp

"Anatalio Ubalde's name is synonymous with successful economic development online strategies. This book benefits from his unique insights, experiences, and storytelling, to give economic developers a way to thrive in an online society. Every economic developer navigating the online world should read this."

—JoAnn Crary, CEcD, President, Saginaw Future Inc.

"My fellow explorer of the new world of web services, Anatalio Ubalde is the perfect guide for anyone bringing their professional activities online. The web has actively connected people beyond any other technology and this book covers the important implications of that change."

—Jan Jannink, PhD, Web Entrepreneur, Investor, and Stanford University Lecturer

"Finally, a comprehensive and complete guide for the professional economic development practitioner on how to conduct economic development online. Ubalde and Krueger explain in easy-to-understand terms what an online rookie MUST do while coaching staff and working with stakeholders in the process of economic development. From websites to mobile applications and soup to nuts, an economic development professional needs this on their desk as the ultimate reference."

—Marty Vanags, CEO, EDC of the Bloomington Normal Area and Economic Development Blogger

"The funny true-stories of online dating and R-rated e-mails make this book both a humorous read and a serious handbook on how to foster economic development victories online. This is not your typical how-to economic development manual."

—April Mason Nichols, Vice President, Spring O'Brien

Economic
Development
Online

Also by Anatalio Ubalde

Economic Development Marketing: Present and Future
Anatalio C. Ubalde and Eric Simundza
2008

Economic Development Online

EconomicDevelopmentOnline.com

Anatalio C. Ubalde & Andrew Krueger

For more information, visit:

Economic Development Online:
www.EconomicDevelopmentOnline.com

GIS Planning:
www.GISplanning.com

ZoomProspector:
www.ZoomProspector.com

ISBN: 978-0-615-40005-1

Printed in the United States of America

10   9   8   7   6   5   4   3   2   1

Contents

Introduction

I was late for springboard diving practice because my meeting at the office ran over, so I was one of the last people on my team to stretch and get on the diving boards. Our team often works out at the same time as college students and youth, and while I was stretching, a precocious 11-year-old girl said to me, "Why are you the last one into the pool?"

"I guess I'm the slowest one," I said.

"Slow and steady wins the race," she responded.

I thought this was cute because she knew the story of the tortoise and the hare. I said "Thank you. That makes me feel better."

But before I could get my last word out she interrupted and said, "But that's not effective in the modern world."

"I guess you're right," I said, more than a little shocked.

She quickly responded, "We have computers now."

☜

I've been teaching about how to leverage the Internet for economic development since the late 1990s and my talks have taken me all over the United States as well as Europe and Asia. I've shared ideas about the latest trends in online economic development with thousands of economic developers in my business travels and I have also learned from them.

While listening to these professionals tell me about their greatest challenges, the Internet is consistently something economic developers want to know more about—more than I could share in the limited time I had with them. They have asked me for additional information so they can effectively implement online strategies and tactics in the office, but all I had to give was PowerPoint decks and links to webinars I'd given. I'm pleased to now be able to share this book as a new resource with all of you.

This book is broad in its larger look at the changing economic development profession, yet specific in its focus on the Internet. It is strategic in using the Internet to achieve economic development goals, yet tactical in describing the online tools to create immediate results. The book includes concepts, theory, practice, tips, data, trends, case studies, how-tos, best practices, and much more.

At its core, however, it is a book of stories. These are the stories of countless economic development friends I've met and their experiences using the Internet. And it is also the stories of how my business partner and I started with a vision for how the Internet could transform economic development; it's the history of how that idea became a passion for the hundreds of economic development organizations that implemented our software on their websites, making our company one of the fastest growing companies in America.[1]

Economic development has always been personal for me because so many of the people across the country that I have had the pleasure to work with have become my friends. Also, like so many of my peers, I take it personally because economic development matters deeply to our society.

This is a book about your stories, my stories, and our stories of trying to understand the Internet and thrive in an online society. *Economic Development Online* is both a guide and starting place from which we can write new and better stories of our communities' economic growth.

Anatalio C. Ubalde
San Francisco, California

Why this Matters

1

The greatest danger in times of turbulence is not the turbulence; it is to act with yesterday's logic.

—Peter Drucker

Surf and Turf

The future of economic development is "surf and turf." To succeed our organizations must be increasingly high-tech and high-touch. The high-tech surfing will happen on the Internet and the high-touch turf relationships will come from deeply connecting with people and companies. Our profession will remain relationship-centric and the personal, high-touch element of our work will be a cornerstone.

Although this book is titled "Economic Development Online," it is actually about both the high-tech and the high-touch, because all of the Internet strategies are designed to lead to relationships that foster economic growth in our communities.

The Internet has Changed Us

Disruptive technologies such as the Internet have quickly changed the way people access information and communicate. This shift is dramatically impacting many industries, including economic development. As a result, many traditional industries have had to adapt because business as usual could spell their ruin. Economic development organizations (EDOs) are not immune from this transformation and are figuring out how to compete in an online business environment. The EDOs that adopt new technologies early for their work and capitalize on the opportunities that new information communication makes possible can create a competitive advantage. Alternatively, those that ignore new technology opportunities will have to play catch-up or potentially become irrelevant. Economic developers must thus ask themselves these important questions: "How is the Internet changing our work, the work of our competition, and the expectations of our customers?" and "How can the Internet help us?"

No Longer a Middleman

People have historically made good livings from being information middlemen and this includes economic developers. They have created value knowing information that was not readily available to others and by brokering transactions.

But the Internet has spurred a new trend resulting in the disintermediation of many businesses such as travel agents, stockbrokers, and car salesmen due to the transparency of information which allows people to go directly to the source. Businesses and EDOs that have adapted to this change have prospered by adding value in new ways, but those that have not evolved are floundering. Successful organizations have adapted to a model in which they freely provide information that will lead customers to want to talk to them and potentially start a relationship.

To receive, you must give first.

The New Rules

Much of what used to work in marketing and communication doesn't work well anymore, if it works at all. We were raised in the "TV-Industrial complex"[2] in which limited media channels like broadcast TV and the big-name, print business publications allowed you to reach everyone because people had so few information consumption options. Today, there are hundreds of specialized channels on cable TV, millions of websites on the Internet, and billions of people entertaining, communicating with, and influencing others online.

Reaching millions of people worldwide through the Internet to tell the story of why your community is the right place to open or grow a business is fundamentally a new opportunity, because to accomplish this before required expensive advertising or media coverage.[3] In addition, if you do a good job telling your story directly, the mainstream media will find out and tell it too.[4] If you want to be effective, you can't use old solutions for a communication infrastructure that doesn't exist anymore. Today, communication, consumption, influencing, marketing, and decision-making are all occurring online and affecting our offline realities.

Your Competition is Adapting to Win

Economic developers are already adapting to the new rules of online economic development. They freely give detailed information and provide Internet tools so that businesses can instantly analyze the benefits of their area. Their websites include tools with searchable databases of properties, site-specific demographic analysis reports, business lists mapped by industry, and interactive mapping tools to identify the best business locations.[5] EDOs that provide these resources are getting called for more information.

Take GlobalWatt, a multi-million dollar solar tech company. Within minutes of using MIGreatLakesBaySites.com, GlobalWatt's site selection consultants were able to bring up and identify two potential buildings—one of which turned out to be ideal for the company. After pre-qualifying the community and sites on the website, the CEO and site consultants visited the community during the weekend, toured the building and met with area leaders in the solar industry. They were impressed with the depth of solar expertise, research, and manufacturing already present in the Great Lakes Bay region thanks to companies such as Dow Corning, Dow Chemical and Hemlock Semiconductor. JoAnn Crary, president of Saginaw Future—the EDO for Saginaw County, Michigan—described the experience saying, "GlobalWatt evaluated sites and found its Saginaw location in one working day utilizing www.MiGreatLakesBaySites.com."

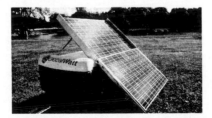

Image 1: GlobalWatt's solar manufacturing goes to Saginaw County.

Site Selection Happens Online

As you will further discover in Chapter 5, corporate real estate site selection is increasingly occurring online. Your area is being considered and selected—or rejected—before you are even contacted. The initial research is occurring online more than it is through personal contact with you, so the importance of your online presence and information is mission-critical. As unexpected or counter-intuitive as it may seem, corporate real estate professionals responsible for site selection say your website is more important as a marketing tool for influencing them than actually meeting with them to personally show them around your community.[6]

The High Cost of Getting This Wrong

With billions of people online and millions of companies using the Internet as a central portion of their activities, you can't afford to have unsuccessful economic development online. It's simply vital to the health of your organization. Creating an effective online economic development strategy requires making an investment.

Research shows that the Internet is the top marketing budget expenditure for EDOs, which makes sense because research also shows that it is the most effective marketing strategy.[7] The information in this book will provide you with the knowledge you need to make educated decisions about how to redesign your website or expand your online services. In addition, it provides you an educational defense so you will not be taken advantage of by IT staff, consultants, or website developers. In Chapter 14, we discuss how to identify the right website developers and Internet strategists.

From Offline to Online

The old way of viewing marketing and communications (Chapter 3) meant that there were many offline strategies and that your website was your only online strategy. Today, nearly all strategies are online and have absorbed many of the traditional offline strategies. Even the most traditional face-to-face activities like trade shows include booths with large computer monitors connected to the EDO's website and special events being streamed live over the Internet.

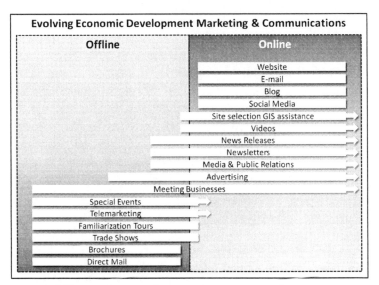

Figure 1: Offline marketing and communications move online.

Evolution

The Internet is transforming our profession in both dramatic and less perceptible ways. From the way that we foster relationships to the way that businesses decide which of our communities are desirable locations for investment, the way that you implement online strategies will impact your success or failure. Online technologies and their usefulness for economic development will continue to evolve. We need to keep thinking about how they will progress and their relevance to our daily work. The following story provides an example of this process.

Story:

Online Dating

I was at a friend's home one evening at a pretty wild party when an important idea popped into my mind. I thought, "This is something I really need to think about and figure out." But at parties like this, there are many people to meet and drinks to enjoy. So instead I drank and visited with other party-goers. Fast forward to the next morning…

I woke up in my bed looking at the ceiling a little groggy from the previous evening. I rolled to my side and saw a woman sleeping next to me. I rolled back over and was looking at the ceiling when the previous night's idea came back to me: "I need to figure out online dating."

So I quietly crept out of bed and turned on my computer in my home office. First I tried using Match.com but you have to set up an account to really experience how it works. It required answering a lot of questions and I didn't have answers for many of them. So I decided I would try eHarmony instead. It had many questions too, and I couldn't really figure out how it all worked. Then I remembered I wasn't alone in my home. There was someone else I could ask. So I went back to the bedroom.

She was still sleeping peacefully, but I decided to wake her up anyway. I nudged her and said "I was hoping you might be able to help me out. I was in my office trying to set up an account for Match.com and eHarmony and I can't figure out how. Do you know how online dating works?" She said to me, "Honey, is there a problem we need to talk about?"

Oh, and there is a little fact of this story that I forgot to mention earlier: the woman is my wife.

You might be wondering what any of this story about online dating and me being married has to do with economic development and the Internet, so I'll explain why it does.

You see, I've been together with my wife so long that I completely missed the online dating experience. Back when I wanted to meet someone to date, I had to do it the old-fashioned way. Even though I have plenty of friends that have used online dating and have even married people they met that way, the technology and process is completely foreign to me.

But I am a technologist and I need to understand online technology because it's my business. Online dating has become a powerful and popular social networking tool and understanding these trends can be helpful to my company and our clients. My wife, however, did not buy this reasoning and told me I better not set up an account on any online dating service.

If you are like me, you may have completely missed out on online dating and are not in a position to need it now. However, I'd argue that you need to understand it and other new technologies for your job. But don't tell your spouse it was my idea to create a dating profile. I mean you need to *conceptually* understand the relevance.

The second reason that online dating is relevant to economic development is because, in the online dating world, there are many great people that could potentially be a perfect match based on their individual characteristics. With the Internet, users can go online and search for that perfect match. Similarly, in economic development, there are many communities that could be the perfect match for a new or growing business. But these businesses might not know which communities are the perfect match because they haven't been able to easily search online to find them.

This conceptual challenge of matching businesses and communities using data search was a fundamental part of the development and design of ZoomProspector.com, the first national site selection analysis website of its kind. You can read more about the creation of this industry-changing website in Chapter 12.

The lesson for economic developers from my online dating experience—or more accurately, my lack thereof—is that we all need to keep up with the online trends. Even if new technology seems difficult, awkward, or confusing, it's crucial to the economic development work we do. Over the many years I've spent teaching economic developers how to best use the Internet to achieve their work goals, I've heard many frustrations and some people have simply dismissed the latest technology altogether. In the early days I was told, "I don't see any reason to use e-mail because it's just not as personal as using the telephone" and "Our department won't let us use the Internet because they think we will waste all of our time surfing the web." More recently I've heard "Twitter doesn't make any sense because I'm not even talking to anyone in particular" and "My office blocked all connections to Facebook because they believe we'll waste all of our time checking out other people's updates."

Today the first two statements sound preposterous. In the near future, the last two statements may seem just as absurd. Some people will always resist change, but your ability to understand, embrace and implement online tools for economic development represents your competitive advantage to seize the opportunity while your timid peers run away from it. To quote W. Edwards Deming, "It is not necessary to change. Survival is not mandatory."

A Brief History of the Internet

2

Revolution doesn't happen when society adopts new technology, it happens when society adopts new behaviors.

—Clay Shirky, *Here Comes Everybody*

The Internet gets big—really big.

The Internet is arguably the only communication medium that is truly global. Accessing a website from a company next door is as close as a website on the other side of the planet. And because it's global, it's very big. According to the Internet World Stats,[8] the Internet currently has 2 billion users, or about 29% of the world's population.[9] North America makes up about 13% of the world's users and enjoys the highest regional penetration rate with 77.4% of its citizens using the Internet.

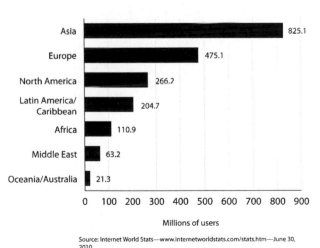

Internet users in the world by geographic region 2010

Region	Millions of users
Asia	825.1
Europe	475.1
North America	266.2
Latin America/Caribbean	204.7
Africa	110.9
Middle East	63.2
Oceania/Australia	21.3

Source: Internet World Stats—www.internetworldstats.com/stats.htm—June 30, 2010

Figure 2: Asia dominates global Internet use.

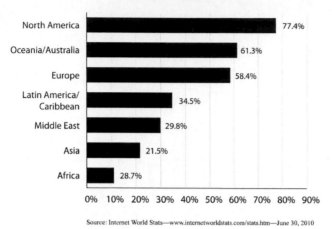

World Internet penetration rates by geographic region 2010

North America	77.4%
Oceania/Australia	61.3%
Europe	58.4%
Latin America/Caribbean	34.5%
Middle East	29.8%
Asia	21.5%
Africa	28.7%

0% 10% 20% 30% 40% 50% 60% 70% 80% 90%

Source: Internet World Stats—www.internetworldstats.com/stats.htm—June 30, 2010

Figure 3: North America, Oceania/Australia, and Europe far outpace the rest of the world in Internet penetration.

The Internet is so big—487 billion gigabytes—that if the amount of digital content were put into bound books, it would stretch from Earth to Pluto 10 times.[10] Even more impressive is that this number is expected to double in the next 18 months. How is that possible you might wonder? Dr. Andreas Weigend, a leading behavioral marketing expert, former Chief Scientist for Amazon, and lecturer at U.C. Berkeley and Stanford University, maintains that due to the emergence of non-voice data applications on mobile phones and an explosion of social networking and media, the amount of data an individual creates is doubling every 1.5–2 years.[11] To add gravity to that statement, he says that more data was created in 2009 alone than all of the history of mankind through 2008.[12]

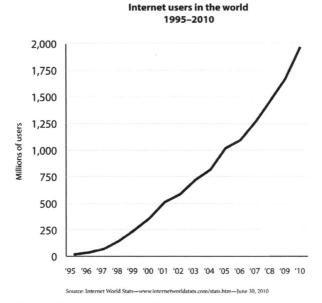

Source: Internet World Stats—www.internetworldstats.com/stats.htm—June 30, 2010

Figure 4: World Internet growth has been constant since 1995.

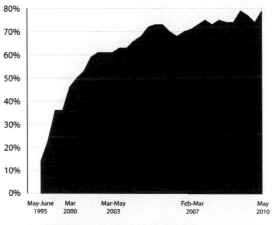

Source: Pew Internet & American Life Project— http://www.pewinternet.org/
Trend-Data/Internet-Adoption.aspx

Figure 5: U.S. Internet adoption has leveled off since 2002, but remains one of the highest in the world.

So the Internet is really big, there's lots of data inside it, and it's growing like crazy. It does sound impressive, but what does it really mean for you as an individual or an economic development organization? What it means is that the Internet isn't just a competitor to other mediums; it's a harbinger of obsolescence. Similarly to the catapult, crossbow, rifle, cannon, tank and airplane, the Internet doesn't compete with its predecessor so much as usher in a completely new era of dominance. It does everything that its predecessors could do, and more. Marc Andreessen, co-writer of Mosaic—the first major web browser—and co-founder of Netscape summed it up: "The Internet's all about software. It can be a newspaper, a magazine, a movie theater or a TV network. The reality is it's all those things."[13] But the Internet isn't just one big glob of existence. It has evolved into the creature it is today. It's worth looking at a few of the big generational leaps that have taken us from early personal websites to ebay, Craigslist, Google, Facebook, and Twitter.

The Internet matures

Web 1.0	The static Internet. Communication is a one-way channel where users browse and engage in simple searches for information.
Web 2.0	The interactive Internet. Communication is two-way and dynamic web pages allow for user-generated content and dialogue among websites AND between users. Users browse, benefit from improved search functionality, and interact with each other.
Web 3.0	An attempt to harness the enormous data unleashed by Web 2.0. Web 3.0, or the semantic web, is an effort to manage the Web's data streams in ways that are meaningful and perceptive to its users.

Figure 6: The Internet's major generational milestones.[14]

Web 1.0 describes the early days of the Internet, when users used the Internet the way that we read a book or a magazine. Information was published; we sought it out, hopefully attained it, and then absorbed it. That was it. End of story. Web 2.0 brought social networks, user-generated content and mobile devices, all of which began dominating web usage, creating enormous amounts of data and increasing the connectivity and engagement between Internet users. Web 2.0 is discussed later in this book in much greater detail.

Much of the emerging Web 3.0 focuses on creating ontologies, which refer to conceptual structures for defining information. Web 3.0 is called the semantic web because it is a way of looking for meaning from elements on the Internet, and having them organize themselves more organically. According to Michigan Tech,[15] the semantic web "provides for a way of using common language to tag data so that information exchange can occur in databases and produce an outcome that's perceptive to the user." Thought-leader Clay Shirky has said: "If I was going to start a news business tomorrow I would start a news business designed to produce not one new bit of news, but instead to aggregate news for individuals in ways that matter to them." Everyone agrees that more structured data is a good idea, but there are still questions about the feasibility of the semantic web. Shirky himself points out that one of the deepest questions of western philosophy: "does the world make sense, or do we make sense of the world?" gets at perhaps one of the fundamental problems of the semantic web. Is it possible to classify and organize such an enormous amount of information? Most experts and thought leaders in the industry believe that regardless of whether a truly semantic web is possible, the Internet will continue to grow and structure its information in a more personalized and meaningful way to its users. That's good for us, because it means that both producers and consumers on the web are going to be able to communicate more deeply and richly than ever before.

Now that we've seen where we came from conceptually, we can dig a little deeper into some actual usage trend data and see where we are today, and where we're headed tomorrow. Who's using the Internet? How are they using it? Which users will be using it in the future? And how will they be using it?

According to the Pew Research Center, certain Internet activities are almost completely commonplace for all users. E-mail, search engines, and consumer research on products are employed by nearly all Internet users. However, social media usage is on the rise as more users begin to post ratings and comments, and consume video and audio online.[16] To learn more about trends in social media, see Chapter 10.

Activity	Percent
Use E-mail	91%
Use Search Engines	89%
Research Products	81%
Research for Job	51%
Rate a Person or Product	32%
Download Videos	27%
Download Podcasts	19%
Source: *Pew Internet & American Life Project*	

Figure 7: 2006–2008 U.S. Internet user activities.

It is also interesting to note that among the 12 to 32 age cohort of Internet users, 52% watch videos online, 35% use social networking sites, and 32% read blogs. Additionally 59% of 33 to 44 year olds use the Internet to visit government websites.[17]

Knowing what activities Internet users engage in is valuable, but knowing how frequently they engage in them also speaks volumes. Figure 8 shows the percentage of Internet users engaging in certain activities at least once a day.[18] Many aspects of the Internet are routine, such as e-mail, search, and social networking, while others are only important at a particular moment (see Moment of Relevance, pg. 20).

Daily Activity	Percent of Internet Users	Last Asked
Use the Internet	78%	May 2010
Send or Read E-mail	62%	May 2010
Use a Search Engine to Find Information	49%	May 2010
Use a Social Networking Site	38%	May 2010
Watch a video (on video sharing site)	23%	May 2010
Visit a local, state, or federal government website	12%	May 2010
Use Twitter or other Status-Update Service	10%	May 2010
Post Comments to any Website	8%	Sep 2009
Look for Info about a Place to Live	5%	Aug 2006
Create or Work on Web Pages or Blogs	4%	Sep 2009
Take a Virtual Tour of a Location Online	4%	Aug 2006
Rate a Product, Service, or Person	4%	May 2010
Source: *Pew Internet & American Life Project*		

Figure 8: Daily Internet activities 2000–2010.

Broadband

High speed Internet, known as Broadband, has also proliferated at a rapid rate. According to the Pew Internet & American Life Project, 74% of all American adults (18 and older) currently use the Internet. Nielsen estimates that among those users, 95% had access to broadband at home and 98.5% at work. By 2013, 99% of all U.S. Internet users are projected to be using high speed Internet at home, while that same figure is expected to be reached sometime in 2011 for the workplace.[19]

Pew's Internet & American Life Project found that increased access to high speed Internet is affecting web users' behavior in the following ways:

- Users become creators and managers of online content.

- Users satisfy a wide range of queries for information.

- Users engage in multiple Internet activities on a daily basis.

The Big Takeaway

- The Internet offers an unprecedented level of communication.

- Through its increasing size and connection speeds, the Internet allows for a wide array of powerful media: video, GIS, interactive databases, social networking, and location aware applications.

- Despite its enormous size, it continues to grow at an even faster rate, eliminating a content ceiling and creating unlimited "shelf space."

Online Communication Trends $\quad$ 3

The Magic Middle

Traditional economic development efforts have focused on reaching three main targets:

1.) The most powerful business decision makers, such as CEOs, presidents, and owners

2.) Site selection consultants

3.) All businesses

It never made sense to target "all businesses," but organizations still tried mass marketing. They either did this because they didn't know better, had money to waste, or both. In case you haven't heard, mass marketing is dead, and even if it wasn't, as economic developers we don't have the budget to compete with multinational companies advertising in the mass market.

However, the other strategies did make sense because you wanted to reach the ultimate decision maker, who was the CEO, or the site selection consultant who recommended the best communities for that CEO to decide on for an expansion or relocation.

In the pre-Internet world this was the way to go because there were a very small number of full-time, professional site selection consultants[20] and you could conceivably meet a sizable share of them individually or at the conferences they attended like CoreNet, NAIOP, SIOR, ICSC, IAMC, Business Facilities LiveXchange, or even at one of the boutique site selection conference gatherings. So you went to meet with them face-to-face, which took a lot of your time—and time, as we all know, is a limited resource for us all.

It also made sense to target the CEOs because you knew the best and limited marketing channels to reach them. They all read *The Wall Street Journal, Forbes, Fortune, BusinessWeek*, and the other leading business publications. So you used traditional public relations to get a story about your community placed in these publications.

But the Internet has changed what communication is possible and how to influence a company to invest in your community. Now your options are much wider and better because you are less restricted by your budget and limited number of staff to target just the most powerful decision makers. Today, with the Internet, you can influence the people that directly influence the most powerful decision makers like CEOs.

At a Web 2.0 Expo I attended, Mark Jarvis, then Chief Marketing Officer of Dell Computers, explained this clearly with a chart (reformatted for this book) that he called "The New Marketing Strategy":

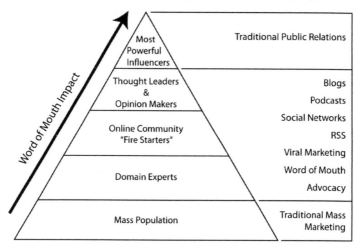

Figure 9: The Magic Middle.

The pyramid represents the conceptual size of the audience with the fewest "most powerful influencers" on the top—usually CEOs—and the "mass population" at the bottom representing the largest possible audience.

The impact of word of mouth increases as it moves up the pyramid to the final decision-maker. Economic developers have primarily targeted only the most powerful influencers and the traditional mass market in the past. But it's the space in between the mass market and the decision maker that is the most ripe for opportunity, because you can really engage in influencing the communication in between.

The *magic middle* includes the domain experts, online community "fire starters," and thought leaders/opinion makers. These are the people whose opinions will most matter and who will influence the final decision-maker about making a business investment in your community. And you don't have to use traditional mass marketing and public relations to reach the magic middle. Instead, an effective way to reach them is through new media including blogs, social media, distributed applications, and viral marketing.

By engaging domain experts in a positive and helpful way such as providing them with convincing data about your community's industries, they can facilitate a favorable review of your area when they write their expert analysis. By engaging online community "fire starters," they are the people most likely to create an online movement promoting your town. Domain experts and the online community both have a tremendous impact on the thought leaders and opinion makers that advise the final decision makers.

Today, in order to influence the final decision makers, you need to influence the influencers in the magic middle. They are easier to reach than the CEOs, they appreciate your interest in them, and they are the people that are respected and relied on. Help them rely on you.

The Marketing Director Becomes a Marketing Coach

It is impossible for the Marketing Director to be the only marketer of your organization in an online society. And this doesn't just mean that everyone in your organization must be involved in marketing and communications. Today, everyone is a marketer including everyone outside of your EDO who is a fan or foe of the work you do. The Internet gives everyone a large marketing bullhorn.

That's why the economic development Marketing Director must be a Marketing Coach. The contemporary Marketing Coach must train all outward-facing internal staff, strategic partners, and community advocates how to distribute information about the organization through all of their collective online and offline communication channels.

Of course the Marketing Director must also continue to direct, which involves developing marketing messages, initiatives, and activities. But the implementation should be distributed through a much larger legion of online voices and partners that can share, forward, like, retweet, and communicate your message.

Moment of Relevance

The Internet, and search in particular, are essential for placing your community's business solution in front of a customer at the *moment of relevance*. This is the unique point at which they have a problem and are looking for a solution. It's when the person moves from not being ready to: "it's time to make a decision."

Businesses have many moments of relevance during their lifetime that provide economic developers with unique windows of opportunity to engage them. These can include business planning, site selection, opening a business, growing the business, expansion to new locations, consideration of closing the business, relocation, or other key moments in a business' life. Each is an incredibly important opportunity for your organization to provide value online at the moment of relevance, because that is when you can create a significant investment impact for your community.

Because the Internet is used as a place to do research and find out answers to questions, it is also where your organization needs to appear at the moment of relevance when businesses are making decisions.

Permission Marketing

In *Permission Marketing*, Seth Godin persuasively argues that the old way of marketing to consumers, interruption marketing (15 second TV ads in the middle of your favorite sitcom for example), is dying.[21] The new way to market to your customers is to ask for permission to talk to them—to give them control, respect them, and let them choose to have a relationship with you.

Interruption marketing worked in part because huge amounts of money were spent on it and consumers had few media options to gather information or consume entertainment. In a restricted model like this, there was no need to do targeted marketing if you could reach everyone. So for decades this method was successful, because the more money people spent bombarding people with advertising, the more money people spent on the advertised products. But the effectiveness of this model started declining when people began having more media choices, and the Internet represents exponential choice. Now, interruption marketing has become just that—an interruption to our lives.

Permission marketing is the opposite of interruption marketing. Customers are in control, not you. Permission marketing still requires that you go after your customers. It still requires your ideas to be fresh and your content to pop; but instead of something generic meant to appeal to the mass market, under Permission Marketing you *earn* the right to market to your customer by demonstrating to them why they are being selected for your message. Using this method, you educate and offer them *real* proof of how they can benefit from what you offer. It's less about generic catch phrases and more about an explanation of exactly what expertise and value you are offering the customer. At that point, the consumer can decide if they're interested and want more from you, thereby giving their permission. No means no, but yes or maybe means that you have started an engagement far more powerful than interruption marketing ever provided. A significant advantage of this is method is that you move your audience from expensive interruption marketing that bothers them, to an educational exchange where they signal that you have permission to continue sharing your message with them. If you have a customer's permission, you have their attention. They've handed you the microphone, and with the Internet, a dialogue between you and your consumer can begin. That relationship can lead to genuine trust and move the customer towards a business relationship.

Unfortunately, the Internet has given economic developers an even greater platform for producing interruption marketing in the form of unwanted advertising and e-mail spam. The advertising that people experience on the Internet desensitizes them to any advertising at all, and software has made it easier for your potential customers to ignore you forever by blocking your organization's e-mails. But the destructive habits of other EDOs are an opportunity for you, because if you demonstrate real value to businesses, you will stand out from all of the irritating EDOs that just keep flooding customers with unwanted advertisements. If you seize the opportunity, the Internet can enable economic developers to educate their customers and tailor relationship-building communications that help solve their problems.

Public Relations

Public relations used to be primarily for the media. If you wanted to get news out, you tried to contact the media to help you get the word out. You begged and hoped they'd find your press release worthy of some of their time or you hired a PR firm to convince them. Those days are ending. The Internet hasn't made press releases completely obsolete (the media is still useful for certain events), but it has changed the way you get your information out.

Today, if you have news, you should share it with anyone who wants to hear it and specifically send it to people who you want to hear about it. Today, instead of press releases, you should use news releases. News releases put your organization in control of when and how you get new information out to your target audience. In essence, as David Meerman Scott points out in *The New Rules of Marketing & PR*,[22] news releases are the convergence of public relations and marketing. You're marketing your organization to an audience and providing a widespread release of information to anyone else who finds it among the channels you've distributed your news. It also loosens the restrictions on the frequency of releases. Because it's so much cheaper than traditional press releases, you can put out many more news releases throughout the year highlighting your expertise, new events, big changes in your community, or anything that you consider to be newsworthy. The content does need to be valuable to a reader, but you aren't restricted to the media's idea of news; you can decide what you release based on your target audience. You can write about pretty much anything that your organization is doing. For example, you could write about:

- A new employee training/re-training program offered by the local community college
- Businesses that are starting up or expanding
- The status of major development or construction projects in the area
- Your CEO/President/staff speaking at an event or conference
- Targeted industries that you are attracting and assisting
- Unique demographics for your community and why they are an advantage
- Trends
- Interesting information to share

Lee Rainie, the director of Pew's Internet & American Life Project, recommends using the 5 As to take advantage of what he calls "a general new pattern of communication and influence for organizations."[23] When writing your news releases, consider the goals of the 5 As:

- **Identify acolytes**
  Find out who your followers are and explore those relationships.

- **Invite attention**
  Send out alerts and updates.

- **Offer pathways to information acquisition**
  Forward quality links and pass along online conversations you've found valuable.

- **Help with assessment**
  Offer your expertise and build your brand.

- **Enable action**
  Provide tools for participation and feedback from your followers.

Riding the S-curve

Economic developers can get success from other peoples' hard work. You can do this on the Internet by riding someone else's "S-curve."

The basic concept, as is shown in Figure 10, is that your organization can benefit from participating in someone else's platform or network that is growing quickly along an S-shaped path during the growth-spurt.[24] By doing so, your organization gets to ride the wave of success as it is occurring. Also, your organization reaps the benefits from all of the work that others did to create the S-curve wave before you joined it.

S-curve

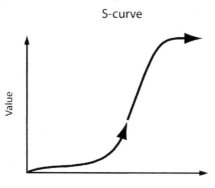

Members of the Network

Figure 10: The S-curve.

There are many examples of S-curves, and within the context of this book, one historical example is the Internet. When the Internet started, the value was limited to just a few people. As more people joined, the value increased dramatically, as did the number of people using the Internet. Today there are new S-curves your organization can ride to success, and I'll share two examples. The first is social media. The adoption of this platform worldwide is massive and by linking yourself to its growth your organization can latch on to its rise. We discuss how to do this in Chapter 10.

The second S-curve your organization can ride is very specific to economic development. Today, hundreds of EDOs are part of ZoomProspector.com, which enables their communities to be found by new, expanding, and relocating businesses, as well as site selectors.

These EDOs have created the critical mass and momentum to make the website successful. You can now ride the S-curve that they built getting all of the same benefits without having to be an early pioneer.

National Trends in Economic Development

4

A national survey of economic developers conducted in 2010 indicates that the website is considered to be the most effective marketing strategy available.[25]

Marketing Strategy	Rating Effective[26]
Website	71%
Out-of-Town Meetings with Businesses	56%
Public Relations	53%
Special Events	50%
Site Selection Consultants and Familiarization Tours	49%
E-Mail	45%
Social Media	34%
Targeted lead Development Databases	33%
Trade shows and Conferences	32%
Slogans, Logo and Identity	29%
Online Video (YouTube, etc.)	22%
Brochures	18%
Online Advertising	18%
Company Blog	15%
Direct Mail	14%
Print Advertising	11%
TV/Radio Advertising	11%
Videos (VHS, DVD, etc.)	10%
Telemarketing	6%
Source: "Budgeting in Crisis" presented by A. Ubalde at the IEDC Leadership Summit, February 2, 2010.	

Figure 11: Economic developers' ratings of marketing strategies.

An economic development website has an advantage over other marketing strategies in that its content is delivered to the right audience exactly when they want it. In the words of one respondent, "Just because our organization is in a magazine doesn't mean everyone reads it. Just because we have a special event doesn't mean that people didn't just come for the free food or booze. But you don't come to a website because it's fun. You come because you are interested in our economic development."

Certain elements of the economic development website have proven to be more valuable to economic developers and are evident from this list of the most important features:

Website Feature	Percentage of Economic Developers Rating Feature as Important
Demographic reports	90%
Labor force	90%
Land/sites and buildings inventory	89%
Maps	86%
Staff directory and contact information	86%
Major industries or business/industry clusters	85%
Infrastructure	83%
Major employers	80%
Incentives	79%
Quality of life	76%
Employment training programs	76%
Site selection analysis assistance	75%
Hyperlinks to other organizations	71%
Business assistance services	68%
Testimonials and success stories	63%
News about community	62%
Comparisons to other areas	56%
Business list	51%
Transactions	45%
Videos	19%
User-generated content	11%
Source: *Economic Development Marketing: Present and Future*	

Figure 12: Economic developers' rating of important website features.

The importance of the Internet to economic development is growing. It is one of the few marketing strategies for which investment increased during the economic doldrums from 2008 to 2010. Different types of EDOs have embraced the Internet to varying degrees, however. Even though the public sector is often thought to lag behind the private sector in terms of innovation, government EDOs surveyed allocated more of their funds to websites than private economic development corporations (EDCs). Also, rural EDOs spent a higher percentage of their budget on websites than urban EDOs.[27]

Perhaps rural EDOs are realizing that they have the most at stake in creating a web presence, as they usually have less visibility and are thus less likely to be visited on a business trip.

The increasing emphasis that economic developers are placing on the Internet does not mean that face-to-face communication is dead or likely to die. Economic developers place great value on conducting out-of-town meetings with businesses, but in the recent economic climate, economic development agencies have trimmed their spending on this activity, as it usually goes hand-in-hand with hefty travel expenses.

As you see in Figure 13, four of the top five marketing strategies EDOs are giving a budget increase are in the online marketing realm: websites, social media, e-mail, and online advertising.

Marketing Strategy	Budget Cut	Budget Increase[28]
Website	6%	43%
Social Media	7%	31%
E-Mail	6%	22%
Special Events	27%	17%
Online Advertising	15%	17%
Public Relations	21%	17%
Out-of-Town Meetings with Businesses	37%	16%
Trade Shows and Conferences	44%	15%
Online Videos (YouTube, etc.)	9%	15%
Targeted Lead Development Databases	12%	14%
Brochures	40%	13%
Company Blog	10%	13%
Slogans, Logo and Graphic Identity	17%	13%
Site Selection Consultants and Familiarization Tours	21%	13%
Direct Mail	30%	10%
Print Advertising	52%	9%
Videos (VHS, DVD, etc.)	18%	6%
TV/Radio Advertising	24%	6%
Telemarketing	14%	4%
Source: "Budgeting in Crisis" presented by A. Ubalde at the IEDC Leadership Summit, February 2, 2010.		

Figure 13: EDOs' budget cuts and increases.

Economic development websites are not only growing, they are evolving. One of the most profound changes is a move from static content to interactive features. In 2008, only a third of economic development websites contained interactive maps and GIS-based site selection analysis assistance. Even fewer contained interactive demographic reports. However, many respondents indicated that they would be adding those features, enough that by 2013, the majority of organizations planned to have added those interactive features to their websites.[29]

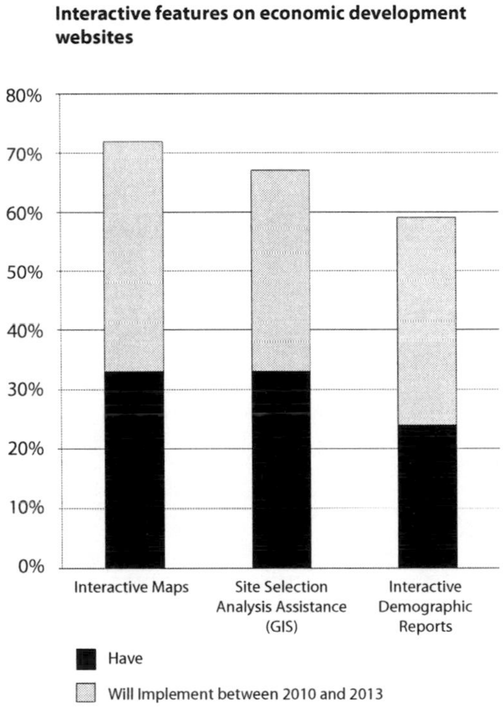

Interactive features on economic development websites

Source: *Economic Development Marketing: Present and Future*

Figure 14: Interactive features on economic development websites.

Even though the website is fast becoming the centerpiece of economic development marketing, most organizations suffer from the same basic problems limiting their websites' effectiveness. 29% of organizations do not possess a website analytics service to track visitors to their websites, and 45% fail to update their websites more than once a month. Alarmingly, 9% of EDOs only update their website one or two times a year.[30]

How Site Selectors are Searching

5

For economic development organizations working with site selectors, how and when site selectors obtain information about communities matters. In another national survey,[31] site selectors were asked when, during the process of site selection, they would first contact an economic development organization and when they would first visit an economic development organization's website. The results showed that 98% of site selectors use the websites of economic development organizations at some point in their research.

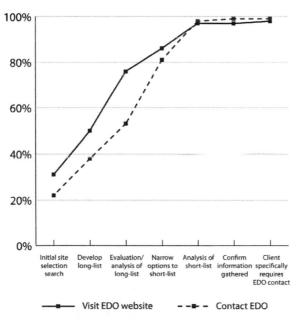

Contact made by site selectors by stage

Source: *Economic Development Marketing: Present and Future*

Figure 15

Figure 15 indicates that *in each* of the first four stages of site selection, site selectors are far more likely to visit the website than make a phone call to the organization. By the end of the third stage of site selection (evaluating a long list of locations), site selectors were almost one and a half times as likely to have visited economic development organization websites than to have personally contacted an organization. This also means that 43% of possible site selector "contact" is lost by not communicating effectively through the organization's website.

This is an important issue, because many communities and economic development organizations are now being eliminated from the site selection process before they are ever contacted, which indicates the extreme importance of an effective website. One survey respondent wrote:

> We often get calls from businesses that are already past the early state of their decision making process because they use our website tools to help them with their analysis. Because of our website our staff now spends more time with qualified and educated businesses instead of people that are just asking simple questions when they aren't even sure if they are going to invest in our community. For example, one business called and I started asking him basic questions and telling him about our community. He said, "I know that stuff. I saw it on your website. I want you to set up a tour for me of three buildings that match what I need that I found on your website."

Organizations that lack effective websites will lose out on the chance to speak to businesses that may be interested in their community. What's more, they will never even know that they lost out because of their website. They will never hear from a prospective business tenant that their website is poor or that they couldn't find what they were looking for—they won't hear anything at all. And unless the EDO uses a website analytics service to track user activity—which many EDOs fail to do—they will not even know that the user was on their website in the first place.

"Economic development organizations still comprise the lifeblood of site selection," says Dennis Donovan. "Once we're down to 10 or 15 potential locations per project, we reach out to economic development organizations before we have to visit local areas to find local operating conditions, such as, what are the expanding companies, water and sewer capacity, electric power reliability, etc."[32] Economic development organizations provide the qualitative information other sources lack.

Case Study:

SeverCorr Steel Manufacturing Chooses the Tennessee Valley

SeverCorr's relocation was one of the largest corporate site location projects in 2005 and was covered in *Expansion Management*.[31] The magazine cover read, "The Internet Puts its Mark on the Site Selection Process—Companies can find all they need for their initial location searches on the Web." Consistent with the trends just described in the national survey of corporate real estate professionals, this is exactly what happened in a high-profile business location process.

SeverCorr LLC searched for 2 years for a state-of-the-art steel assembly plant and thought it found the right site in Arkansas, only to discover that new utility regulations made the location too costly. After tucking his kids into bed for the evening, Eddie Lehner, SeverCorr's CFO, was on the Internet and went to TVA-sites.com. From the comfort of his home computer he used the Tennessee Valley Authority's GIS site selection analysis website and identified all the pertinent information he needed to find his company's future location. "We're in the cradle of our marketplace. There is good proximity to our end-user markets…All the important components of a site are there [on the website] for you, [such as] incentives, transportation, and work force," said Lehner.[32]

According to John Bradley, Senior VP of TVA Economic Development, "By leveraging the power of the Internet and GIS for economic development, we are expanding our networks through TVAsites.com to generate more leads and secure more projects in the Tennessee Valley region."[33]

As of 2011, $900 million have been invested in the Phase I, 1.2 million square foot plant. It employs 545 workers at an average annual salary of $72,000. In addition, $200 million of a planned $500 million, were recently invested in Phase II construction of the plant, which will increase employment by 93.[36] The company produces high-quality steel for automotive and other purposes with plans to do business with companies like Honda, Hyundai, Nissan and Toyota. Geographic analysis mattered when considering the location and the website was an important factor in choosing the location. The power of quick access to the MegaSites listed on the website saved SeverCorr LLC nine months in the location process.[37] Economic development officials estimate that companies moving into the region to leverage SeverCorr's high-grade steel could total over 1,000 additional jobs.

TVA's website was also being used by Wal-Mart to sell the large vacant stores in its real estate portfolio. In addition, information from the website was also used in the proposal that led to Toyota building a manufacturing facility in the Tennessee Valley. The $1.3 billion manufacturing plant will employ up to 2,000 people and be used for the manufacture of Toyota's Highlander sport utility vehicle.

"Business success is often influenced by making wiser decisions faster than your competition. Through the Internet, TVAsites.com puts the information businesses need to make a site selection decision at their fingertips. It is a tremendous value to the business community," said Heidi Smith, General Manager and Marketing Director of TVA Economic Development.

Fam-Tours

Familiarization tours, also known as "fam-tours", have been a traditional way in which economic developers invite corporate real estate professionals and site selection consultants from around the country to visit their community. This typically involved flying the consultants out, providing accommodation, touring the area and potential development sites, presenting information about the community, wining and dining, and relationship building. It's a big event requiring the coordination of site selectors traveling from around the nation, local business people, politicians, and community ambassadors. It's often very expensive for the EDO but many find it to be worthwhile and valuable. The site selection consultants often need to be paid to attend these events by the EDOs because being out of the office is time they can't work on paid projects and, as important as it is, they can't find the time to visit every community just for the education.

The converse version of the fam-tour is when the economic development group takes a tour across the country meeting with the consultants in their own cities or travels to a particular city and then goes from office building to office building meeting with several corporate real estate pros over a day or two.

There are plenty of advantages and disadvantages of the traditional fam-tour or visiting consultants at their place of work. The relationship building and personal time are valuable but the cost and planning are monumental.

An untapped opportunity that economic developers should experiment with is having virtual familiarization tours with corporate real estate professionals by leveraging new advances in Internet technology. Progressive site selection experts like Deane Foote have already warmed to the idea of web-based tours of communities because it saves time and travel.[38] Imagine doing a fam-tour in which, on your side of the web conference, you have all of the same people you would have on a traditional tour, able to speak at the right time to the consultant. You could use polished digital presentations to show the key concepts you want them to remember. Instead of a long drive in the cold of winter or heat of summer, you could use video to show them around your community and development parcels more quickly than driving. Through the video you could highlight some of the very best things to see about your community. You might think this is digital cheating, but you do the same thing in real life, because you know you don't take them down certain roads in town.

There are some clear benefits to virtual tours:

1.) A web meeting will cost a few dollars or a few pennies depending on the service you use. That's a lot less than flights, hotel accommodations, etc.

2.) You can do a lot more web conferences in one day from your office than you can face-to-face. You could literally have web conferences in which you start your first fam-tour on the east and follow the sun as it moves west scheduling several meetings in one day when before you could only schedule a few face-to-face.

3.) You could record your live web fam-tours and create on-demand familiarization tours for corporate real estate pros in the different industries you are targeting. They could watch them on your website on their own schedule. And other corporate real estate pros that you never even considered meeting with might benefit from the video and lead to additional prospects coming to town.

Video conferencing is certainly a new technology and a novel way of doing fam-tours. Although it will never be as personal as a face-to-face meeting, don't discount it just because it's a different type of communication. I'm sure that when people had the first opportunity to make a phone call, they said it wasn't as personal either. But today we don't fly to see people every time we need to talk; we call them. Maybe that's the future of fam-tours.

What to Put on your Website

6

The average economic development organization already has many features on its website and plans to add more enhanced features, especially interactive tools like GIS site selection analysis, testimonials, and comparisons to other areas. The following figure shows what EDOs had on their website when the survey was conducted and what they plan to add over the next few years.

Website features and items

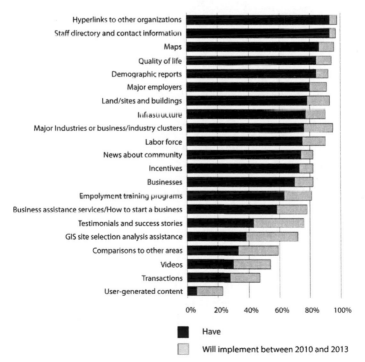

Source: *Economic Development Marketing: Present and Future*

Figure 16

There are many things you should include on your website and this section of the book begins the process of detailing some of them. Some elements are quickly described because they should be self-explanatory, others have some more explanation, and new or more sophisticated online tools are covered in greater detail, often in their own chapters.

Contact Us

Put your contact information, including all of the information you would put on your business card in the "contact us" section of your website. This seems obvious, but even today too few organizations do this. Sometimes they just put a contact form for someone to fill out which gets sent to no one in particular.

Your website should enable people to contact you in every way that is appropriate including traditional forms of communication like phone, fax, e-mail, and mail. For mail, use a street address, not a PO Box because some overnight delivery companies don't deliver to PO Boxes.

Include contact information for each person in your office that you would like the public to be able to speak with. Ideally this would include their job title or responsibility so a website visitor will know the right person to contact.

Your website can also provide direct links to the social communications your office uses for work, such as Twitter accounts, or their professional profiles on websites like LinkedIn.

Demographics & Community Profile

The demographic and labor information about your community are the two most important things to have on your website according to national research.[39] They even surpassed available properties, maps, and the organization's contact information.

So these must be on your website in a way that is easy to find and which provides robust information. It is even more desirable and useful to businesses if they can access demographic and labor reports interactively and for different market areas and distances by address or around available properties.

This data needs to be extremely current because Census data is often too old to be used for important business decisions. Companies don't want to make a $100,000 decision based on outdated data, let alone a multi-million dollar investment. It is best to use current-year data whenever possible, and there are companies that specialize in providing demographic projections.

Demographic and labor information can include, but should not be limited to, detailed data for population, sex, age, race, households, income, unemployment, housing units, household size, and educational attainment.

EDOs focusing on retail businesses should include consumer expenditures or retail spending.

Industry & Business

A business considering an investment in your community needs to be able to understand the type of business environment that they are joining. The local businesses may be customers, vendors, competitors, or partners.

Include detailed information about the industries in your area including business establishments, number of employees, establishments by size, major employers, companies by industry, employees by industry, employees by occupation, and labor rates.

It is preferable if businesses can analyze industry data geographically and use search to find business lists interactively.

Other Community Characteristics

There are many other characteristics that will be of interest to different types of businesses. When targeting specific industries, provide the information that matters to them. Examples of these types of other community characteristics include utilities, transportation, telecommunications, taxes, quality of place, climate, education, parks, outdoor activities, nightlife, public transit, healthcare, culture and art.

Business Assistance

Probably one of the most commonly asked questions is: "What can you do to help me?" Explain the assistance, services, programs and incentives your office can provide. This section could also include information about services that your county, region or state provides.

It's fine if your neighboring communities provide similar or the same assistance. They might not be promoting all of their assistance and you will look comparatively better if you look like you have more assistance available. Multiple assistance programs also provide the company with a broader selection of potential programs that can serve its needs.

Starting a Business

Whether starting a business in your community is easy or difficult, providing a road map through the process helps. This checklist can let a business understand the steps that are necessary to open its doors for business. This can include listing the departments that the person will need to visit such as business licenses for a license, the planning department for construction, or any specialized approval required for a unique business. Contact information can be provided for utilities and business assistance organizations.

Small Business Information

The types of assistance small businesses require are unique. Often there are small business development organizations that help with writing business plans, find financing, and provide small business workshops. Let the small businessperson know what resources are available through your office or other agencies. Links to other small business assistance organizations can also be listed.

Employee Training Programs

If your community has employee training programs, list this information as well as the contact organization providing the services. Qualified employees, or employees that your community will train to be qualified, are a great asset to a future employer. Let a prospective company know that these services are available.

New Business Developments

Prospective businesses, existing businesses, and residents like to know what new business developments are occurring in your community. Prospective businesses want to see the business environment they may join. Existing businesses want to know that the place they have joined is continuing to be a successful place for business. Residents want to know what is happening in their community. Don't forget that if your own residents think your city is a good place for business they will tell others—and there are a lot more citizens out there to promote good news than there are economic development professionals in your office.

Promoting new business developments on your web site, and online, can be accomplished in many ways. Newsletters or e-mail newsletters can be posted on your website chronologically. You can also write your own news releases and blog posts about economic activity in your community in the form of new businesses openings, commercial construction, promoting local businesses that are doing well or are expanding, and infrastructure improvements that will help the business climate of your community. Blogs and news releases are covered in Chapters 3 and 10.

Planned Economic Development

Let people know where your community is going. What is your community's vision of its future? Some businesses like to be in a growing community while others like consistency. Are there major new projects in the works or have you limited new construction? What types of businesses are you planning to attract and grow? Where have your elected officials or board of directors directed your team to focus your time? This is another area in your website or blog that allows you creativity in describing your future community. No one knows exactly what the future will look like—but this is an opportunity to paint the picture of what your community wants to be.

Maps

Do not assume that everyone knows where you are. Providing a map helps orient people to better understand how your community is laid out and where streets and major locations are found.

Although a local map is beneficial, a regional map is also valuable. It will place your city within a larger regional context. This is important because a company may be interested in locating in a region such as a state, county or metro area. By positioning your community as an excellent place within this region you increase your likelihood of inclusion and consideration.

If your community is considerably less known than some of the larger cities, it may help to include a large-scaled map showing your location as a point within your state on a national map.

Adding interactive maps is easy today and many of the online map services provide an Application Programming Interface (API) to embed maps into your website. Many EDOs are also adding interactive GIS maps with economic development data analysis which is further described in Chapter 7.

FAQ

Many web pages have a FAQ (Frequently Asked Questions) page because it saves the staff and visitor time. Often, the questions the user has are the same questions everyone else has. In your case, these may be typical economic development questions ("What incentives do you have?") or questions specific to your location ("What benefit is there to locating in your Empowerment Zone?"). By answering these questions before they are asked, you will save yourself time and help educate the site visitor.

Links to Appropriate Organizations

Your hyperlinks to other organizations should be links to your partners in economic development. They are the organizations to whom you would refer your website visitor. Examples could include the Chamber of Commerce, economic development office, regional economic development organization, or small business assistance agency. Do not list every link you can think of because this only confuses the user and hinders them from finding the most important resources.

Geographic Information Systems & Site Selection

7

In God we trust. All others bring data.

—W. Edwards Deming

The most prominent "killer application" designed for economic development websites came from the addition of Geographic Information Systems (GIS) for site selection analysis. What started with a few organizations has become an industry standard that the majority of organizations either have or will have in the next few years (Figure 14, pg. 31).

GIS is essentially the connection of digital maps and spatial data-bases to perform powerful analysis. It's the uniqueness of each community's geographic characteristics that makes it a better or worse place for businesses to start-up, expand or relocate. Because EDOs promote location advantages, GIS is the ideal tool for helping convince a company why it should invest based on quantifiable and comparative data.

A business may also have fundamental questions it must answer during a site selection project to determine if it can succeed in your community:

1.) Is there a physical place to locate the business such as an available building or developable land?

2.) Who are the people living and working in the area and what are they like? These are potential customers and employees.

3.) What businesses are in the area? These are potential customers, partners, and competitors.

4.) What are the geographic business advantages? These can range from access to transportation, markets, tax incentive areas, colleges, amenities, and more.

Prior to having on-demand site selection analysis on an economic development website, the process of gathering this information often took weeks or months to collect and resulted in inconsistent and general data. However, by adding GIS to the economic development website, it shortened this process to just a few minutes and delivered location-specific analysis through reports, pictures, maps, graphs and analysis that were reliably high-quality. This represented a huge time-savings for economic development staff and a competitive time-to-decision for private companies making a site selection decision, which is one of the many reasons this technology has become a must-have for competitive EDOs.

The following images show the logic and steps that businesses and site selectors go through during the process of finding the right location in a community using an EDO's website:

Image 2: A business enters the property and location requirements.

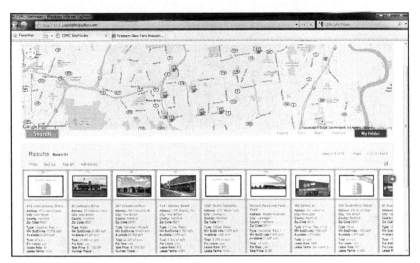

Image 3: All of the matching properties are shown as a list and on an interactive map.

Image 4: The report shows property and contact information with pictures below an interactive map.

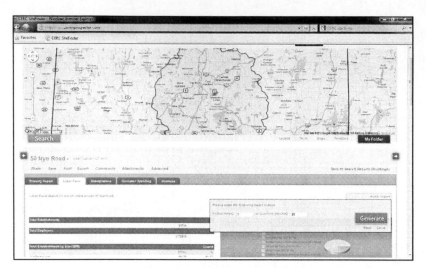

Image 5: A location-specific labor force analysis of a user-defined driving distance is created. Other reports include demographics, consumer spending, and wage data. This provides market research to the business to identify the optimal location to access quality employees, customers, and other market considerations.

Image 6: Businesses are mapped by industry to show the spatial concentrations and locations. Data such as the number of businesses and employees in each industry are summarized below. By clicking on an industry the website visitor can view the names and information of individual businesses. Also, website visitors can narrow their analysis to show only a particular industry or to narrow their search within the industry by variables like revenue or employment.

Image 7: Demographic data is displayed as a heat map showing the spatial variations of population, income and other variables.

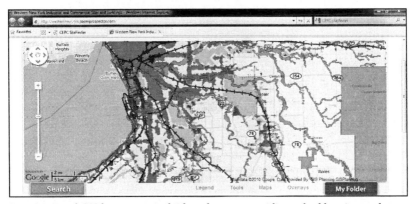

Image 8: Local GIS layers are overlaid on the map providing valuable primary data such as zoning, incentive areas, traffic counts, and more.

To see live website examples of cities, regions, and states implementing this technology, visit GISplanning.com.

The Tipping Point for GIS

Today, web-based GIS are implemented by EDOs in nearly every state and serve the majority of the 100 largest cities in the USA as well as thousands of other communities across the country.

A recent national survey of economic developers shows that between 2010 and 2013, web-based GIS site selection will become a tool that most EDOs have on their websites. In 2008, 33% of EDOs had web-based GIS and by 2013, another 34% planned to add the technology, bringing the total adoption for the industry to 67%.[40] Well past a tipping point, the minority of EDOs without the technology will find themselves at a competitive online disadvantage. Due to competitive pressures, GIS is moving from a "good-to-have" to a "must-have."

Case Study:

Dell Uses GIS to Come to Oklahoma City

In 2004 computer manufacturer Dell was undertaking an international site selection project to locate a customer care center which was scheduled to employ about 3,000 workers. The company was considering 122 cities in North and South America.

Dell eventually chose a 60-acre site in Oklahoma City for a new 120,000 square foot facility. The new facility was scheduled to result in approximately $4 million capital investment and an expected cumulative overall economic impact of $764.7 million. After a three month search to choose the final site, the Greater Oklahoma City Chamber's web-based ZoomProspector GIS tool played a key role.[41]

"It was a good tool to use to determine what properties were available," said Peter Kaharl, Senior Manager, Corporate Real Estate and Construction, Dell Inc. "It made the process easier because I could go in there myself and look at it. A picture of the site also helped put a reference point with it. The ability to seek a match for Dell's specific requirements for the project, along with being able to obtain data associated with properties such as cost per square foot and availability in Oklahoma City, was particularly nifty. Every search has its unique characteristics," Kaharl said, adding that OKCedis.com helped in finding the land and amenities needed to support the project. "We looked at hotels, places for people to eat, traffic conditions around the site now and at the time we will occupy it."[42]

Image 9: Greater Oklahoma City Chamber's site selection application, OKCEDIS. com.

One of the data requests Dell made of the chamber was labor force data within a specific drive-time of potential development properties. Although Dell was expecting to receive the data in a few weeks, the Chamber was able to use the website GIS tool to create the data in minutes.[43] Although the data was one component of the overall site selection effort, the response gave an impression of the professionalism, speed, and quality of service Dell could expect from the Oklahoma City team.

Brenda Workman, former Director of Central City Development for the Chamber noted that "In just 30 minutes we were able to generate a report from www.okcedis.com for about three sites in the Oklahoma City workforce draw of 19–39 year olds. We were able to generate a report, email it to the company, and they were able to make a decision on which site had the best workforce draw. The company was blown away with our response time and the accuracy and efficiency of the data."

"The www.OKCedis.com tool has created tremendous value for our organization and for our corporate real estate partners in the region. When you combine the ability to search for any available property in the region with sophisticated demographic and economic data…we provide a higher level of service than almost any other region," said Roy Williams, President of the Greater Oklahoma City Chamber of Commerce. "We understand that in today's environment, companies don't have the time to put together data from a multitude of sources," Williams said. "If we can centralize data into these web-based programs and provide greater access to information analysis, we can compress days of research into minutes."[44]

OKCedis.com maps the locations of properties, provides searchable demographic profiles, shows the location of existing businesses, and displays additional layers of information such as traffic counts, parking, Business Improvement Districts, land use, Enterprise Communities, Enterprise Zones, Empowerment Zones, and NSRA Boundaries.

Local businesses looking to expand like QuikDrop also experienced the benefits of OKCEDIS to identify the right site. "It was late one night and I found the www.okcedis.com website from my home computer. The website was one of the main reasons for choosing our company's particular location. Using the website we were able to match our business demographic to a location with the best value," said Robert Walker, Owner of QuikDrop, an eBay Power Seller. "I tried many places on the web to find the necessary information, but the Chamber's website was the only one-stop-shop for every type of data we needed in both the raw data and geographical forms. It made it so easy to present it to headquarters for their approval of the new business location," Walker said.

Image 10: Dell Customer Care Center Under Construction in Oklahoma City.

Story:

Creating Innovation in Economic Development Websites

The inspiration for the first web-based GIS for site selection came from my work in local economic development in the Bay Area in 1997, and my extreme dissatisfaction with how ineffectively I was working with businesses interested in opening in our city. I would get a call with a business' requirements and then have to call multiple real estate agents to figure out what properties were available, followed by rounds of phone-tag. Next I would compile standard demographic and labor data about our community, try to add some local information about their industry if I could find any, walk from city hall to various departments asking for additional information, and then add a full-color brochure with the name of our city in a font from the eighties. To put this all together could take days or weeks depending on who I was still waiting on to deliver the correct information. I knew what showed up in their mailbox wouldn't convince me to grow my businesses in town and I doubted it would convince them either.

I was new to the profession, having just finished grad school, so I asked other peers in economic development if this was the process they also followed, and they told me, with some variations in their work, that it was. So I knew the process was broken. But I knew it didn't have to be this way and I had an idea how to fix it.[45]

There were three trends that were very relevant to my work at the time. One was the concept of reinventing government. Another was that GIS was becoming more accessible through GUIs (graphic user interfaces) and you no longer needed to program in UNIX to make it work. And finally, there was a new technology that seemed to have a lot of promise called the Internet.

What we did was leverage all three of these trends to solve our problems. First, government was broken. Second, economic developers weren't using GIS—which had the capacity to be an ideal location promotion tool. And finally, the Internet provided the opportunity to efficiently centralize data and decentralize access to the largest possible audience of businesses.

On June 24, 1998 our project launched and it was *The Wall Street Journal* that broke the story saying, "The site offers a host of geographic, demographic and economic information often sought by companies and site selectors."[46]

Like any major innovation it was met with excitement from other economic developers who had suffered the pain of a broken system. It was also met with scorn and ridicule from some established professionals.

The problem with changing the status-quo with a better system is that some people have a lot invested in the old way of doing things. Change could be risky for them because they might need to change, which could threaten what currently was working for them. I collided into this problem in a public and humiliating way.

I was invited to speak at a national training on marketing because the organizers had heard our new program was getting a lot of buzz. I spoke the first day and the talk was met with enthusiastic excitement from the attendees because of the possibility of implementing a similar program in their communities.

The next day a well-respected consultant spoke about the site selection process and what economic development professionals should do to be successful. A few of the attendees asked about how parts of the site selection process would change in light of the new website program recently launched in my city, which other communities wanted to implement. Although she wasn't very familiar with what we did, she dismissed it and said that I couldn't possibly know what to do because I was too young and inexperienced. And, in front of the whole audience, she plopped down a book about site selection and told me I should read it so I could learn something.

It wasn't quite the debut I was expecting for my first national talk on the subject, but there was something that both she and I could learn.

My blind spot was that there were probably many people making a good living with the way things were and a change to that represented risk. I didn't consider that because I was relatively new to the profession, didn't have anything invested in the status-quo, and didn't care if the old way didn't work if a new way would. But that was my mistake because not everyone is ready to upgrade and I wasn't sensitive to these types of dynamics. So I suffered her insult because we had just started the program and it had resulted in only a few successes in the first months of the program. At this point it was more like a novel idea than a movement. But while I was being jeered, I kept thinking about a Victor Hugo quote, "All the forces in the world are not so powerful as an idea whose time has come." That was her blind spot. (There is a very happy ending to this story, which is that she is now a friend of mine and has even recommended our software to communities she has worked with. I think she's terrific.)

In 1998, GIS Planning's software was implemented in one state, in 2000 four states, in 2001 it doubled to eight states, in 2002 it doubled again to 16 states, and today we have projects in 42 states, and serve the majority of the largest 100 cities in the USA and thousands of cities across the nation.

I wasn't quite sure exactly when our movement, which was really led by local economic developers, would reach a tipping point of becoming a mainstream industry must-have, but there were three anecdotal moments worth mentioning.

The first was when the copy-cat products arrived with low-quality offerings from people who saw we invented something important and wanted to get in on the revenue stream. A few weeks before I discovered what he was doing, an owner of one of these imitation-product companies literally said to me during a dinner, "I want to be like you." I didn't realize just how much.

However, if people are just in it for the money, they aren't in it for the passion, and that's a long-term business liability. When our technology was invented, I happily worked on a modest government salary, in an office cubicle with a view of a brick wall, because I loved economic development.

At one level these other companies are just trying to make money from our innovation. At another level, every copy-cat company trying to ride our coattails simply validates the concept that we invented and fought to make a success. We continue to innovate and lead which is why over 95% of the people who have selected an online GIS site selection system select GIS Planning.

Our first clients were all medium-sized cities and our heart will always be with smaller sized communities. But over time the largest cities and regions in the country implemented our Software as a Service too. The second moment came when recognized leaders of our profession coming from these big cities talked matter-of-factly about our software as something they *had to have* based on the expectations of businesses and corporate real estate pros. That was powerful because we realized that our solution had crossed over as a needed solution for communities of all sizes and that our software created an expectation.

The third moment was when research showed that within the next few years the majority of economic developers planned to have GIS site selection implemented on their websites. Although it hasn't happened yet, it's already all across the nation. And we continue to have the faith that it's an idea whose time has come.

Some of the lessons we learned from these experiences, that have helped shape our company and which I hope you future economic development innovators will learn from, are:

1.) If you have strong convictions, follow your passion no matter what the critics say. If you are going to be an innovator, then realize that not everyone will see your vision immediately. If you focus on creating value, they will see it eventually. As Henry Ford said, "If I had asked people what they wanted, they would have said faster horses."

2.) You can work with the status quo, disrupt it, or both. Understanding industry dynamics and sensitivities can be keys to unlocking change.

3.) If you have a winning solution, don't be deterred by imitators. Just keep focusing on creating value for your customers and you will always succeed.

4.) Love your work. Help others succeed.

Online Proposals & RFPs

8

Proposals and Documents

The ability to create documents interactively based on existing website content has been around for years. The simplest version of creating a document is to create it from static webpages from an EDO's website which can then be e-mailed to a customer. This just turns web pages into document pages, by reformatting them to be printed and perhaps adding a table of contents or other graphics. A more sophisticated method of creating documents is through the creation of interactive webpages such as the results of a user-created property, business, or demographic search and then taking those interactive results and reformatting them into the printable document.

However fancy this concept may initially appear, it's actually not innovative. It's regressive. What is happening is that the highly interactive power of the web is being denigrated into a format without the web's power, just to create a printable document off-line. But as a concept it could be appealing to an economic developer that values information in the form of atoms (paper) instead of bits (web, mobile).

This is not to say that printable documents aren't important, especially because paper is something people are familiar with. Instead, they are going to become obsolete over time as people become more comfortable benefiting from the interactivity of online documents which they can bring with them anywhere through multiple devices, all of which will be Internet accessible nearly everywhere. And this reality isn't very far off at all. For example, I used a wireless Internet connection for my laptop and smart-phone on a plane trip for free and I was sitting in coach. This will become the norm, not the exception.

The future of proposals and documents is the online document which can be created from your static, dynamic, and interactive content. Instead of printed pages you can only read, the online proposal can include video, interactive maps and GIS analysis, slideshows, spreadsheets the person can modify, links to other detailed documents and much more.

The online proposal that is interactive already exists and a number of states and communities are already leveraging this communication and education strategy as you will read about next in RFP and Proposal Management.

RFP and Proposal Management

If you have ever worked for a statewide economic development organization and have been responsible for managing an RFP in which you have to collect responses from dozens of communities within your state and then compile all of those responses into one proposal for a company, you have experienced a special kind of suffering.

First, you have to notify all the communities, even those that probably shouldn't respond because they aren't a good location fit, because you have to be fair to everyone. Then you receive all of the responses at different times and in different formats with many of the responses being incomplete and in three-ring binders. And finally, you have to put them all together through a weird process of editing using scissors, tape, and a copy machine to create a final document that looks more like a scrapbook than a site selection proposal.

As creative as this arts-and-crafts method was, the Internet has provided a more efficient and effective method for managing RFPs and creating final documents. Today a number of innovative states have taken the process online. Instead of the previous method, the state is able to issue the notice for the RFP to all their economic development partners through their RFP management system, which is only accessible through a unique login and password process to its economic development partners. Because it's available to all partners equally, it creates a level playing field of access. Then, the communities can submit all of their properties through the states' sites and buildings system, upload digital documents in support of their submissions, and include any additional files for their proposal. All of the information from each of the communities ends up in one system location and is all digitally editable so the state can easily manage the submissions.

The state can then subtract, add, or edit the content and push only the desired information into a single online proposal for the customer. The document is available with read-only information in a printable format or is available as an online proposal with interactive access to detailed property reports, site-specific demographic analysis, interactive GIS mapping, and communication directly with the economic developers. The whole proposal can even be sent as just one hyperlink.

The first EDO in the USA to implement a system like this was the State of Oregon, but today many more are using it, such as Indiana, Oklahoma, Massachusetts, Wisconsin, Connecticut, Minnesota and more. The following image is an example of a portion of an online proposal; however, all of the confidential information has been censored to protect the privacy of this statewide economic development organization.

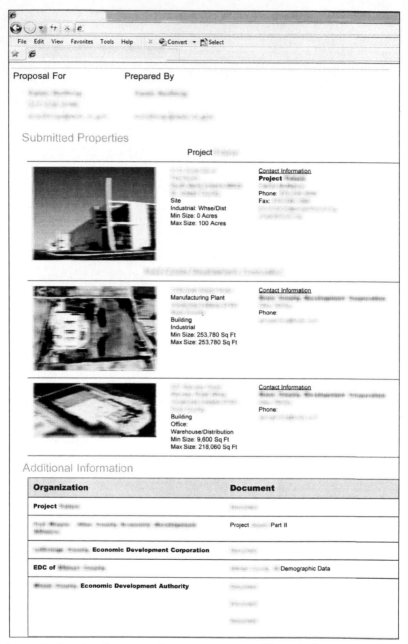

Image 11: Sample online proposal summary page. Confidential information has been blurred.

Searching Local Businesses 9

B eing able to search for, analyze, and visually present your local businesses are important features to have on your website. An obvious first reason is that by making your local businesses searchable you provide the opportunity to promote the companies that support your economy today. Local people can use this tool to find businesses they can shop at, hire services from, or with whom they can create business partnerships. However this is something that Internet users can do on a variety of other websites including Google, Yelp, CitySearch, and YellowPages.com. It's not to say that providing this similar business search feature on your website is redundant, but you aren't likely to be a first-source destination on the web for this type of search.

So instead, add to your business search in ways that these larger online business directories are not focused. The way that you promote your local businesses can be much more than just finding their address or phone number.

By adding additional data and search parameters to your local business search you can greatly enhance the information about your community's businesses and industries. For example, you can search for businesses by industries and provide summary data about the cumulative industry such as the total number of employees and revenue, and also map the locations of all of these businesses on an interactive GIS map that shows the geographic concentrations spatially. Or you can provide the ability to search for a series of industries with related supply-chains or clusters so businesses can analyze the interconnectedness of your industry clusters.

Adding these types of tools is not only valuable as an internal tool for your EDO's planning and analysis, but it is also an excellent way to enable outside companies to better explore and understand the benefits of your business characteristics.

These new ways of searching for local businesses are implemented on a variety of state, regional, and local EDO websites. For specific examples you can go to EconomicDevelopmentOnline.com.

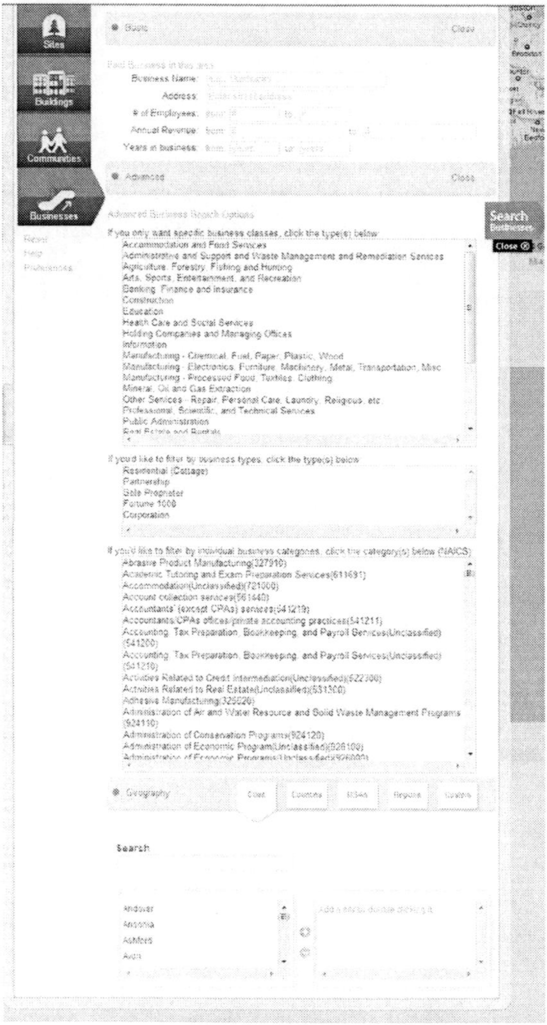

Image 12: On this business search website, the user is able to precisely search, list, and map businesses based on the business name, address, employees, revenue, major industry, detailed industry, and user-defined geography.

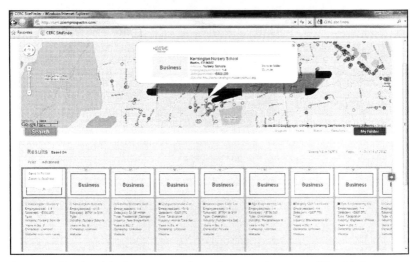

Image 13: Results of the business search are shown on the map and listed below.

Tip:

Business Directories

Although business directories from large Internet companies like Google, Yelp, Bing, CitySearch, and YellowPages.com aren't necessarily things to put in your website (although in some cases you could using their Application Programming Interface), it's important to be aware of these services because they impact your local businesses being found on the Internet.

As consumers increasingly start their search for businesses online, the effectiveness of your local companies being found on the Internet will affect their bottom-line success. Your EDO can encourage your local businesses to be aware of methods to be found online and even provide training.

In addition, many of the business directory websites include customer reviews of the companies. This means that businesses need to monitor the websites that their companies are listed and what people are saying about them.

Online directories like Yelp and CitySearch are already go-to websites that millions of people use to search for and decide which businesses to patronize. Search engines like Google, Yahoo, and Bing also have reviews which come from direct review posts or aggregated reviews from other websites.

One of the interesting tools available to local businesses is Google Places. It enables businesses to claim their listing on Google and provide additional information about their companies such as the hours they are open, what credit cards they take, pictures of the establishment and more. Companies can even provide coupons and specials for people that click on their Places profile. As Google Places provides more information to businesses and customers it will increase the potential benefits to both groups.

Social Media   **10**

 S ocial media is a term that's thrown around in a slew of different
situations; however, there's nothing complicated about social media at its core. It is simply another platform for communication and
relationship building. Social media is also grass roots and works on a
pull model, where only people who have something of value will get
"followers" and an audience. This means that to engage your audience, you must always focus on providing value. Despite the bells
and whistles of technology, social media's value at its core is human
beings being social—this will never change, no matter what evolves
technologically. It's a value that we've possessed for a very long time
as humans and social creatures; the Internet is just helping shape the
way we do it.

Social media is in a similar position to the Internet in the 1990's.
Many are ready to acquiesce to the fact that it's important and has a
lot of power, but a solid chunk of the population still feels awkward
about it, thinks it's for kids, and just isn't sure how to effectively participate in social media.

Let's take a very brief look at why social media on the Internet is so
powerful—realizing the fundamental power behind social networks
and their core value can be very helpful for understanding social media.

First, the two graphics on the following page visualize how social
connections inside a network grow at a faster rate than the number
of users when networks grow larger. If only one person has a fax machine or a telephone, it's basically a paperweight. If two people have
one, they have added value to their network because they can share
information. If twenty people have telephones, and can all share information, their unique potential connections have increased from 1
to 190, which is far greater than the rate increase in users (10x).

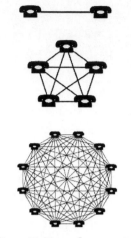

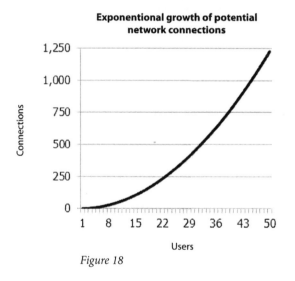

Figure 17: Network connections

Figure 18

Metcalfe's Law, named after Robert Metcalfe, co-inventor of Ethernet, refers to the even greater value added to networks as they increase in size. Metcalfe's Law states that the value of a network is proportional to the square of the number of its connections. The idea is visualized on the following page. Take a look at the number of users on these graphs; perhaps some of them approach the number of people in your e-mail lists or address books. Now consider that Facebook has over 500 million users today and is growing rapidly.

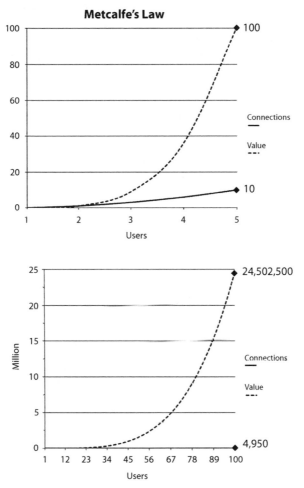

Figure 19: Metcalfe's Law predicts quadratic network value gains per added connection. 5 users (10 connections) receives a potential network value of 100, but 100 users (4,950 connections) allows for a potential value of 24.5 million.

If we compared the potential of all of Facebook's users being connected to each other vs. the potential of 100 people being connected to each other through e-mail, under Metcalfe's Law, Facebook's network would be more valuable by a factor of 637,690,029,078,665,00 0,000,000,000. That's just under 638 septillion if you were counting.

Of course these are potential network connections, because we know that all of Facebook's 500 million users are not connected to each other. In fact, networks often look more like the example below where sub-clusters break off rather than all connect to each other:

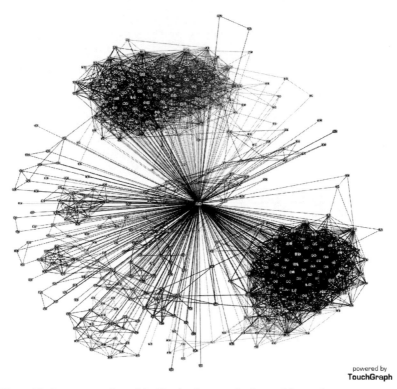

powered by
TouchGraph

Figure 20: A representation of the Facebook network of one of the authors.

There is debate about the validity of Metcalfe's Law, but there's no doubt at all that the power of social networks increases quadratically as the number of base users increase. Keep this idea in mind as we look at ways for economic development organizations to leverage social media.

A recent study by Nielsen shows that social networking, a form of social media, is (by a long shot) the primary Internet activity in the world. It's seen a staggering growth rate of over 43% in just the last year. Recall Andreas Weigend's claim that more data would be produced in 2009 than all of human history through 2008. This increase in social media is the main reason why. Another social media format, online video, also saw a significant increase of 12%. A large part of this is expanded growth, but some of it is also at the expense of more traditional communication channels such as e-mail and search which have declined or stagnated.

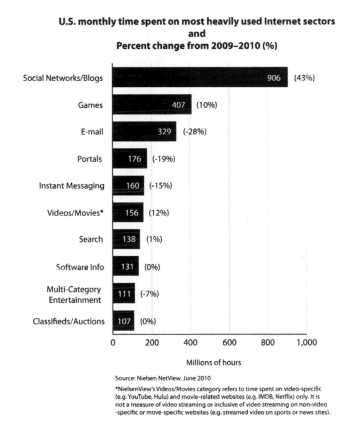

U.S. monthly time spent on most heavily used Internet sectors and Percent change from 2009–2010 (%)

Source: Nielsen NetView, June 2010

*NielsenView's Videos/Movies category refers to time spent on video-specific (e.g. YouTube, Hulu) and movie-related websites (e.g. IMDB, Netflix) only. It is not a measure of video streaming or inclusive of video streaming on non-video -specific or move-specific websites (e.g. streamed video on sports or news sites).

Figure 21: Social networking and blogs are dominating users time and growing at the same time.

13.5 minutes of every hour spent online is dedicated to social networking or blogs according to Nielsen. That's more than double the amount of time on e-mail.

That's why it's important for you to care about social media. Social media is where your customers spend time and can be reached. It's not just for kids; it's now unequivocally mainstream. Facebook's highest growth age group is 35+ and Twitter's is 45+. According to the Pew Center for Research, in the last year, social networking use has doubled in the 65+ age category and grew by 88% among adults 50 to 64.[47] Those numbers show staggering growth and prove that the age gap is closing in social networking.

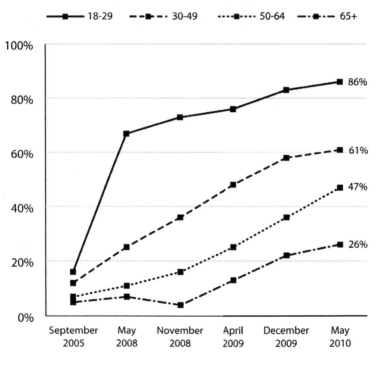

Percentage of adult Internet users who use social networking sites

Source: Pew Internet & American Life Project

Figure 22: Usage among users 30 and younger still reigns in social networking, but older users have seen significant gains in the last few years.

There is an inherent value to these media; otherwise, why would so many people use it so regularly. That value makes for an excellent tool for market intelligence and for making valuable connections to prospective customers and businesses. The bottom line is that social media is happening and people are talking about your community, whether you like it or not. Most likely, they are saying some bad things and some good things, but if you're not using it, you won't know. If you are, you'll be able to make the most of that positive feedback and turn it into something even better. You'll also be able to rectify mistakes or at the very least apologize and offer better assistance with your customer base. You'll also be able to scout out new territory and expand your base. Social media is being included into Google, Bing, and Yahoo search engines to give more real-time query results related to social media. Social media is like word-of-mouth on steroids. It's digital, which means it stays there and can be copied at zero cost.

Josh Bernoff, of Forrester Research, says that the gravity of social media is so unequivocally strong at this point that you should be:

- Convincing your boss this stuff is for real, and that if you haven't jumped on it, you're late.

- Profiling your customer base, and seeing what they're ready for, *before* planning a project to reach out to them.

- Segmenting your audience; building different strategies for different segments. Social Media is so prevalent now that a single approach for your company is probably too broad.

This may all sound overwhelming. But you don't have to jump straight into the depths of social media; in fact, it's better that you don't. The name of the game online is social capital, and you want to build and spend yours wisely—just like you do with your high touch relationships. There is etiquette to social media, and you have to earn your reputation. That being said, as long as you are respectful and customer-centric—listening and responding to those users who own the conversation—your reputation will be sterling. The following diagram shows different types of social media users, ranging from creators of original content, down to listeners (inactive just means a lack of manifested production, not a lack of use). That's an important distinction, because the first rule of being an economic developer in social media is to listen. Take some time to listen. Find out what kind of social media your audience uses and what they use it for. Are they more active and among those on the higher rungs of the ladder? If so, cultivate and encourage their efforts. You can promote it, engage them about it, and respond with input if it adds value, but always listen. If your customers tend to be at the bottom of the ladder and mainly take in information, start producing some for them to take in.

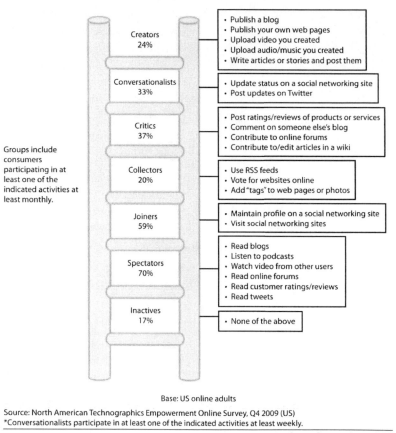

Base: US online adults

Source: North American Technographics Empowerment Online Survey, Q4 2009 (US)
*Conversationalists participate in at least one of the indicated activities at least weekly.

Source: Forrester Research Inc.

Figure 23: Social media users are a diverse group. Not everyone plays the same role and it's to your advantage to climb the ladder from the bottom up.

Once you have a good feeling for your audience and customer base—where they spend their time online and what they converse about—start making contacts of your own (e.g. partners, colleagues, and customers).

After you've started up a small network of relationships, concentrate on defining your goals for your new social media campaign. Think about how you can attract and retain new businesses as well as enable local business expansion. Tap into growing businesses and help them. Add valuable content like tools, tips, and access to information. If you are generous, they won't forget you. If you concentrate on being authentic and providing a service or solution to users inside social networks, you'll be respected for thinking of others first. While the assistance you provide may lead to a business asking for your help or considering an investment in your community, don't over-promote. That behavior has limited appeal in social networks. Social media has a very strong ecology and users appreciate helpful information and consider it a service.

Finally, monitor your progress. Doing so will help you realize some sort of value for your campaign and you may be able to construct a ROI calculation to measure your gains. Use the goals that you set to help drive your metrics. If you're concentrating on attracting new businesses, consider measuring the number of conversations and passalongs, sentiment analyses, and retweets. If you're trying to retain businesses, measure how many followers you have and what proportion are local businesses. Do you have their ear when you communicate? Don't forget to always be conscious of the business health of your local community, logging qualitative needs as well as trying to quantify it through polls. This information can be invaluable in the future.

Remember, the goal is not simply to have the most followers or fans. You need to engage and activate your followers.

Your Social Media Identity

Web 2.0 practices came about from a need to move away from static websites and limited one-way communication in the first decade of the Internet that defined Web 1.0, where the website published information and the visitor simply read that information—very similar to a printed magazine or newspaper. The advent of Web 2.0 technologies, however, not only enabled websites and their visitors to interact, but also enabled visitors to interact with each other, mainly through comments and ratings. Web 2.0 also introduced the concept of User Generated Content (UGC), where the website visitor and not the website owner adds the content. This has added tremendous data and value to the Internet as can be seen on websites such as Wikipedia.org.

Although commenting, ratings, and User Generated Content exploded in Web 2.0, a large proportion of that content was anonymous. For websites where actual business relationships are important, such as economic development websites, there are many problems with engaging in a discussion with an anonymous poster, not the least of which is that it makes the development of a relationship nearly impossible.

In the more recent versions of Web 2.0, in the form of social media, people's online identities have become more authentic because people have online identities just like they have offline ones. For example, your LinkedIn profile is really a representation of who you are, including your own picture, where you've gone to school, and the places you've worked. When you post an update or make a comment on a LinkedIn group, you are making that online post as a real person and it influences your reputation.

Because of this new opportunity, people are spending significant amounts of time marketing and building relationships through social networks like Facebook and LinkedIn. However, there will be some challenges for you as an economic developer in managing and maintaining relationships in social networks.

Most social networks are designed to fit one niche. LinkedIn is for business, Facebook is for your personal friends, and Ning is for special interests. So even if a professional has time to work within multiple social networks, they have to create different profiles and connections and may even have to adopt different personas (i.e. casual, professional, expert) in order to get the most out of these different networks. Also, you will need to spend time recreating or duplicating the networks you've built on one social network into another.

Social Portability

Niche social networks are becoming less siloed as open social standards are being created, but if the market leaders like Facebook don't agree to participate, it is questionable if these initiatives will succeed. There is also some limited ability for users to bring their social capital with them. For example, market leaders like Facebook and Google have Facebook Connect and Google Friend Connect, so that you can bring your Facebook profile with you automatically into their partners' websites, but not their competitors' social networks. Social media is still too new to see how these dynamics will play out. But until there is more resolution, as with your offline relationships, you may have to go to multiple venues to network with different audiences.

Facebook

They are the universe.

—Angel Investor Ron Conway, on Facebook

The Basics:

Launched in 2004, Facebook is the largest social networking website, and boasts 550 million users spending over 700 billion minutes per month on its site.[40] Facebook has seen rapid growth over the last year and passed Google in the first quarter of 2010 to become the Internet's most-visited website.[49] 50% of its users login daily and the average U.S. user spends more time on Facebook than Google, Yahoo, YouTube, Microsoft, Wikipedia and Amazon combined.[50]

What's more, Facebook is expanding at a faster rate than ever before, both as a website on its own, as well as in terms of its connection to the Internet as a whole. Facebook recently launched social plugins—such as Facebook "Like" buttons—that let users see what their Facebook friends have liked, commented on or shared on websites across the entire web.[51] This "Open Graph" initiative is perhaps the most wildly successful initiative so far. While it took Facebook Connect a year and a half to be implemented across 250,000 websites,[52] over 50,000 websites had implemented the new Open Graph social plugins within one week of launch.[53] A mere two weeks later, that number had doubled to 100,000 websites.[54]

What this means is that Facebook is gathering an unprecedented wealth of data about its users that even Google does not have. What's perhaps even more interesting is that when users "Like" a website, it starts to show up in Facebook's search results, with links back to the website.[55] This creates perhaps the most viable competitor for Google than ever before in the history of the search industry.

Facebook Profiles

The most well-known component of Facebook is the profile, which includes news feeds from both your "friends" (contacts) and pages that you "like," via the Facebook Wall and Status Updates.

The Facebook Wall, which is located within each user's profile, is the primary form of engagement on Facebook. Status Updates enable your friends and pages that you have "liked" (thereby subscribing to news about that page) to keep you posted on news about them. People can engage with these updates by "liking" or "commenting" on these posts, creating the opportunity for a type of social dialogue that requires very little time investment. For example, you may not have the opportunity to talk to an ex-colleague or your favorite company, but by "liking" something that they post, you can easily generate some social capital with them.

For your own personal profile page, you can add work and education information about your background on the "Info" tab to add more depth about who you are, along with pictures, videos and applications. This enables not only your "friends," but also the people signing up for your organization's public page to click your name to learn more about you.

What Economic Developers Need To Know:

Facebook Pages

While most users are familiar with personal Facebook profiles, Facebook also allows public figures and organizations like EDOs to create Facebook Pages. While Facebook profiles are for personal social use, Facebook Pages are designed for public figures and organizations. In order to create a page for your organization, you must have an active profile. If you create a page for your organization, you will become the "page administrator" for that page, and people can connect to your personal profile as well.

> **Tip:**
>
> **Facebook Privacy**
>
> If you are concerned about mixing your personal Facebook profile with your professional Facebook page, you can take advantage of Facebook's extensive privacy controls to make components of your personal Facebook profile private or "friends-only." We recommend that you always adjust your privacy settings as Facebook generally sets the most open settings as their default.

Facebook pages are indexed by search engines, giving your prospects and potential customers a new way to discover your community. You can encourage businesses and residents within your community to "like" your page in order to stay abreast of current events within your community, and as a way to stay connected. In order for a Facebook Page to be successful, you must provide a consistent flow of content, with regular updates and prompt responses to ongoing conversations. One goal of your Facebook page can be to create buzz for your community by promoting local events, information, and new businesses. In fact, the content strategy for your Facebook Page should be focused on what is most appealing about a given region and what is most important to its residents. The Facebook Page for your community can be a great platform for seeking out that feedback.

The City of Danville, VA and the Economic Development Corporation of Sarasota County, FL are examples of organizations that maintain a vibrant user base by providing relevant content updates and responding actively to everyone that engages with the content on the page. Posts regarding local businesses and fun suggestions can help draw repeat visits, as can posts showcasing local fairs, events, and current affairs.

Facebook Applications for Economic Development

Savvy economic developers can also leverage Facebook applications to further engage users, and help both local and prospective businesses understand the benefits of establishing their businesses in the region. Many organizations leverage their Facebook Pages to cross-promote other marketing efforts. For example, South Valley Economic Development added a "Join My List" tab to give users an additional way to enter their e-mail address for more updates.

Image 14: South Valley Economic Development adds a Facebook tab for e-mail subscription.

Once you have a Facebook Page, you can boost its draw for the denizens of Facebook by allowing them to view your community demographics and search for properties within your area. This is remarkably simple and easy to implement using a pair of free applications developed by GIS Planning, which can both be found by searching for "ZoomProspector" on Facebook itself.

The demographics application is a way to provide visitors to your Facebook Page with the information they are seeking. To install, simply enter the name of the geographic area that your organization represents. This will create a new demographics tab at the top of your page, providing a wealth of statistics about your community that will be of value to anyone wanting to know more about your area. Whenever these statistics are updated on ZoomProspector.com, they will automatically be updated on your Facebook Pages as well.

The property search application similarly installs a new tab at the top of your page, which will appear beside your existing tabs for your Wall, Info, Photos, etc. You can set the geography that you want to allow the users to search and GIS Planning clients can set their geographies based on the names of their organizations, while all other users can specify a particular city or county. Users who visit your Facebook Page can then access the new property search tab, where they will be able to view featured properties in the area that you select. They also will be able to specify criteria for a commercial property search, including property type, size, and whether they are looking for properties for sale or lease. Running a property search will return a list of properties, allowing users to explore each property and perform detailed analysis of the surrounding area.

Obviously, Facebook has come a long way from its beginnings as a mouthpiece for college kids. These applications can help you tap into the medium's real potential for economic development.

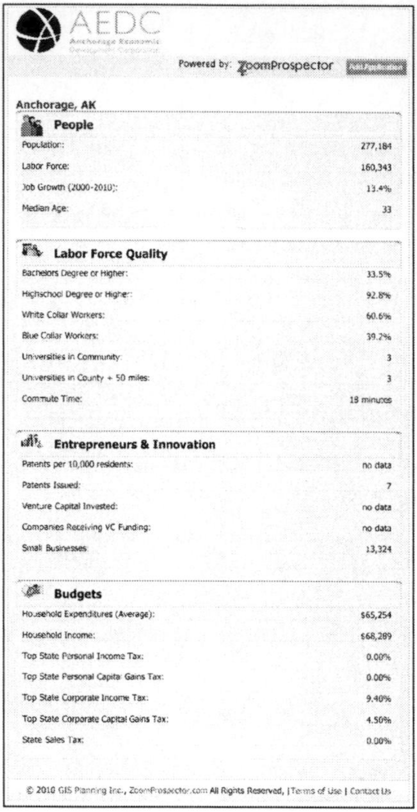

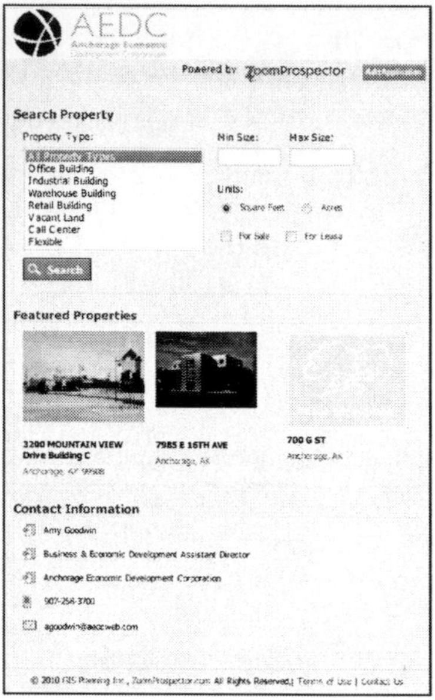

Image 15: ZoomProspector's Facebook applications add tabs for property and demographics.

Story:

How an Economic Developer was Fired Because of his Facebook Profile

Privacy is dead, and social media hold[s] the smoking gun.
—Pete Cashmore, CEO of Mashable

As was previously mentioned, social media is new and therefore the rules and expectations related to it are highly dynamic. It is certainly blurring or shrinking the distance between the private and the public as well as the personal and the professional.

One economic development executive was fired from his position after members of his board of directors were notified of images on Facebook of that executive apparently drinking alcohol and partying heavily. He was not partying in the office or during work hours, he was doing these activities in his private life, but he was fired just the same. The justification from the board was that, as the leader of the EDO, he represented the community in whatever he did and that they felt his behavior was not acceptable as a leader in their community.

There are some important lessons to be learned from this. The most obvious is that the Internet can really impact your job and your supposedly private life that exists online can be accessed and made public. Another is that the culture of technology may be moving faster than boards of directors know what to do with.

You may think that this person was a fool for posting these types of pictures on his profile. But that means you assume that *he* posted them. One of the most important features that made Facebook successful was the ability to take pictures and tag other people in them. When they are tagged it means that the photo shows up on their Facebook wall and profile photos without them ever approving the tag. So if this economic developer didn't check his Facebook account for a few weeks to un-tag the photos they could be available to anyone of his connections he allowed to see his photos.

This technological explanation to the board of directors may not have saved his job, because they could simply say that they don't care and they don't want a leader that parties heavily. This board of directors probably didn't understand the social-cultural elements of this technology. But the deeper problem is that they weren't compassionate enough to understand that people have private lives, history, and everyone has moments from their past that they would prefer were not made public—especially on the Internet.

I doubt that there was one member of the board that hasn't had

> one too many drinks and embarrassed him or herself. If someone took a picture during a compromising moment it could show up any time on Facebook—and as karmic justice maybe it will.
>
> We all need to better understand how Internet technology and social media is changing our lives and how our private lives can become very public. Within this context we could certainly all benefit from being compassionate toward others, because some day the victim could be us.

LinkedIn

The Basics:

LinkedIn has over 75 million members in over 200 countries. While it took nearly a year after its launch in 2003 to attain a 1 million member base, the last 1 million took just 12 days.[56] Today, LinkedIn is the premiere professional social network based on social engagement and building upon real relationships between working professionals.

Given its professional emphasis, the conversations, networks, and content distributed on LinkedIn provides greater legitimacy for businesses. Moreover, LinkedIn is increasingly moving towards a social model, integrating more Facebook and Twitter like features to enable rapid engagement and the establishment of credibility. Its focus on allowing people to showcase their professional expertise and influence makes it one of the most prominent platforms for talent search, career development, and interaction with potential business partners.

There are numerous examples of working professionals landing jobs, businesses raising venture capital, connecting with clients, buyers, suppliers and talent via LinkedIn. The value of this professional social network is no less pronounced for the economic development industry. With numerous economic development oriented groups, company profiles and networking opportunities, LinkedIn provides a vibrant and growing environment for the creation and fostering of relationships that are essential to the goals of an economic development organization.

What Economic Developers Need To Know:

LinkedIn Profiles

Unlike Facebook profiles, LinkedIn profiles are a representation of people's professional reputation—online living resumes so to speak. An Internet search for any established professional will likely surface their LinkedIn profile, and no talent search is complete today without an evaluation of the skills, experience and recommendations listed on LinkedIn.

LinkedIn is thus increasingly the single most important platform for working professionals to showcase their professional and corporate snapshot with tools like executive summary, skill sets, educational background, past and current employment positions, professional recommendations, relevant links, and the integration of news feeds, Twitter accounts, and career-focused applications.

The value of the LinkedIn network is further compounded by the fact that LinkedIn extends your network beyond your own personal connections to the networks of your connections, making it that much easier for people to find relevant business leads and partners that they would not otherwise have access to. For example, while you may only be "connected" with 8 people, your network may expand to 78,000 people due to the size of your connections' networks. This means that 78,000 relevant and targeted professionals suddenly have visibility into your profile, thereby allowing you to increase your reach.

Company Profile

In addition to providing working professionals with a means to showcase their professional background, LinkedIn also enables organizations, such as your EDO, to provide an overview of their services, employees, and location. The company profile feature allows prospective clients, future talent, and potential business partners to get a preview of your organization and its mission before approaching you. LinkedIn supplements the company profile that you create with data about your company from around the platform. This means that all your job listings, links to current and former employee profiles, new hires, and recent promotions are quickly aggregated, giving interested parties a rapid snapshot of the important and recent events relevant to your organization.

In addition to data provided by members of the organization, LinkedIn does its own analysis of your organization and the connections that your employees have on the network. For example, LinkedIn automatically calculates interesting statistics such as your organization's median age, gender breakdown, top schools, and other corporate connections. For job seekers of the future, this provides unprecedented visibility into the structure of your organization.

People can also choose to "follow" your EDO's Company Profile to keep up with updates on your organization. This is also a tool that you can use that enables you to follow companies in target industries or even discover new job opportunities at other EDOs.

LinkedIn Groups

In addition to providing professionals with the platform to showcase their background and skill-sets and corporate affiliations, LinkedIn also allows users to create and engage in groups. There are many active economic development groups within LinkedIn, ranging from large and exclusive national groups like the International Economic Development Council (IEDC) group, to highly specific economic development groups based on specific regions, such as the Buffalo Niagara Enterprise group.

LinkedIn groups provide an important opportunity to engage directly with people within your specific industry, giving people yet another way to establish their credibility and expertise. For example, the Economic Development Leadership group on LinkedIn was started in an experiment to see how many people would join simply by word of mouth. In less than a year, the group grew dramatically and is one of the largest economic development groups on LinkedIn today. Economic developers suddenly have an organic new channel to engage with each other in conversations pertaining to current economic development challenges and issues. Many otherwise unknown or unconnected economic developers can leverage this platform to showcase their knowledge, expertise, and experience with each other, providing the opportunity to create a community of economic developers who are helping each other learn and grow from each other.

For economic developers seeking to build a network, they can simply join this vibrant community and participate in group discussions by either asking questions or providing their expertise and thoughts in existing conversations. As is the case with other social networking environments, your success and prominence within groups depends on the value generated directly and indirectly—either through your responses or by posting thoughtful and relevant questions to spur discussion. Group members have the ability to rate your posts, and LinkedIn automatically ranks posts that spur conversation and engagement by evaluating how many people comment on and "like" that discussion (type "Economic Development Leadership" into the LinkedIn search box to find and join the group).

As with real life interaction, LinkedIn groups are forums for professionals to ask and answer questions, where respect, helpful comments, relevant questions and answers go a long way to establish credibility and create real connections between people. If you post current and relevant discussions, you will be perceived as an authority within the industry, and other economic developers will seek you out based on this established expertise. The image below is taken from the Economic Development Leadership Group Discussion page.

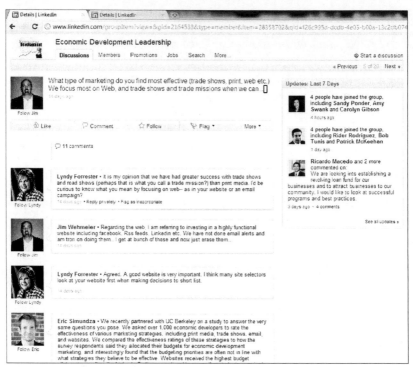

Image 16: Economic Development Leadership LinkedIn Group Discussion Page.

Your EDO can also create its own LinkedIn Group to engage local businesses and companies outside of the area with an interest in your community and organization. Your LinkedIn group can be used to engage with businesses as well as share relevant economic development information that they can pass along through word-of-mouth around town. For example, if there is a local business expanding that needs to hire, this is a way for local people to tell people they know that might be a good fit to apply. Or, if there is a new program your organization is considering you can solicit feedback without a more formal process or focus group. A post like, "How can our community support entrepreneurs?" may return dozens of ideas from the community and reveal issues that could produce a better strategy.

Twitter

The qualities that make Twitter seem inane and half-baked are what makes it so powerful.[57]
—Jonathan Zittrain, Harvard law professor and Internet expert

The Basics:

Twitter is a social networking and microblogging service that launched in July 2006. With nearly 100 million users, Twitter has grown 347% in just the last year.[58] Twitter is also often one of the least intuitive social networking platforms for new users. People often ask, "What is a "tweet" and what is the point?

"Tweets" are text-based posts or "status updates" of no more than 140 characters allowing users to share "What's Happening?" in their world. The concept of a status update in Facebook is essentially a "tweet"—answering the same question of "What's Happening?" While both Facebook and LinkedIn allow for a two-way channel of communication, Twitter was the first to popularize the concept of real time interaction with the entire world. In fact, it is important to note that Twitter has had a strong influence in making both these networks more social and real time.

What Economic Developers Need To Know:

Twitter Profiles

Before you begin, decide whether you want to create an account for yourself as an individual, or your organization. Then, decide on a relevant Twitter username. For example if you decide to create a Twitter account for your organization, choose one that pertains to your organization and region, so that you make it easy for prospective businesses or residents to find your organization on Twitter.

After setting up an account, you will be prompted to create a profile. This profile is an important opportunity to represent your organization. You can only enter a 160 character biography, forcing you to be succinct. You can add to your Twitter profile by creating customized backgrounds using an editor such as Photoshop to provide additional detail about your organization. You should then add a picture that is consistent with your online presence, and add a link to your website to provide more information about your organization's background.

Following/Followers

Most Twitter accounts are public, meaning that these posts can be viewed whether someone is following you or not, simply by going to your Twitter page. However only people who "follow" you (essentially subscribe to your posts) will be able to receive your posts within their Twitter feed. Likewise, you can only view the content of someone's Twitter posts in your own Twitter feed if you "follow" them.

@UserName

The @ symbol is essentially a user (or organization) name on Twitter, for example @ZoomProspector. If you want to direct your public tweet towards a specific person, simply add their name (@username) within a tweet. This is the most basic way to "talk" directly with any Twitter user, because all tweets with their username show up automatically in their @username feed.

RT or "Retweet"

When you "retweet" someone's post, you are essentially telling your entire list of Twitter followers that you think their post is worth repeating verbatim. "Retweets" are a great way to generate social capital.

The key to being successful on Twitter, as with on any online social network (or even an in person conversation, really) is to generate value for your listeners. Providing engaging content, being relevant to what your followers care about, and having an approachable and consistent manner provide people with a reliable stream of content.

Many economic development organizations use Twitter to reach out to a broader audience, and to extend the reach of their content. @MetroDenverEDC is an example of an economic development organization that leverages Twitter to reach out to their audience. They provide news about events, respond to local businesses and residents, and communicate the activities of their organization to their audience.

@AboutDCI is an organization that specializes in "marketing places" and leverages Twitter to provide relevant industry news, promote or "retweet" news from their followers, and share job opportunities via Twitter. Other economic development organizations leverage Twitter to provide a forum for local businesses to advertise special deals, share tips for things to do in the region, and promote local events that matter not only to businesses within the region, but residents who want to know up to date information about their local area.

Case Study:

Combining Traditional and New Media

As discussed in Chapter 3, new media can create a wave of attention that breaks through to traditional media. However traditional media attention can also lead to new media success.

An example of this occurred when EPB, a city-owned utility in Chattanooga, Tennessee announced that it would be offering Internet service of up to one gigabyte per second on September 13, 2010. EPB hired Development Counsellors International (DCI) to conduct a public relations campaign around the news.[59]

The morning of the announcement the front page of the business section of *The New York Times* had the headline, "Fastest Net Service in U.S. Coming to Chattanooga."[60] By the afternoon the story had been covered by the *AP, CNN, Yahoo News and Finance, Huffington Post, Engadget* and other outlets.

The announcement rapidly spread in the social media world. Within the first 24 hours the story was tweeted about 5,302 times, shared on Facebook 4,506 times, generated 1,343 comments on the publications websites and received 9.8 million social media impressions.

Ryan Shell, DCI's Director of Social & Digital Media, used both traditional and modern tactics to gather the data into a social media report. "When it comes to doing things like tracking the total number of tweets and Facebook shares, I gathered that data manually. The report included a sample of 1,500 tweets about Chattanooga that had been published in the 24-hour period after the news broke. It would have been nearly impossible to compile all of that data without utilizing a modern day social media measurement and monitoring tool. These tools are highly analytical and should be a part of any marketer's toolbox," said Shell.

Here is an example of a tweet sent by the official Twitter account for *Wired* magazine, which had approximately 600,000 followers at the time, "@freudianslip99 1Gbps?? Makes me consider moving to Chattanooga."[61]

Video

The Basics:

Between October 2008 and October 2009, 109 billion minutes (a 169% increase) of YouTube video was watched in the US alone.[62] In May 2010, Americans conducted 10.1 billion search queries on Google.[63] In that same month, they watched 14.6 billion videos on YouTube.[64] Video doesn't show any signs of letting up in the near future either. Cisco forecasts that by 2014, it would take more than two years to watch the amount of video that will cross global IP networks *every second*; to watch all the video crossing the network that year would take 72 million years.[65]

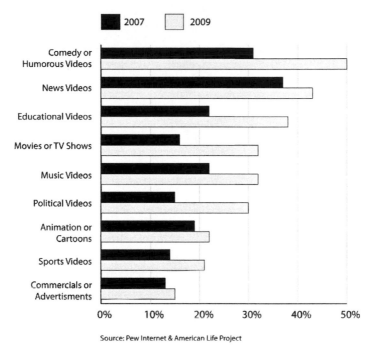

Percent of online adults watching videos by type

Source: Pew Internet & American Life Project

Figure 24: Online video consumption has increased across the board.

What Economic Developers Need to Know:

Video is enormously powerful and intuitive. We're human beings and we're very social creatures. Seeing an actual face of a real person engages us in a way that simply reading information fails to capture. When your organization presents a video to your business community, users who may have passed over more mundane written content will take a look at a video because they don't have to lift a finger. They can sit back and watch—you bring all the content to them and they don't worry if they've missed a link or looked at the wrong chart because you're there—a real face and human presence—to explain exactly what each fact or figure means. Presenting information about your organization via video is not only extremely effective; it's extremely easy to produce as well.

You can host your videos on your own website or blog, or take advantage of online video sharing sites like YouTube and Vimeo. They have made uploading your video a simple, pain free experience. There's no video conversion to deal with in most instances—you just find your video file and hit "upload." You can produce multiple videos on your own "channel," which provides users with a direct link to all of your videos. What's more, you can embed videos from those video sharing sites into your own website while still capturing the social media benefits of having your video reach a wider audience and possibly going viral.

Tip:

Viral Marketing and the Power of 1.1

You've probably heard of "viral videos" or forwarded an e-mail story that you thought was interesting to several friends. But you can also create viral economic development marketing, communications, groups, video, and more.

It doesn't matter what type of marketing you are doing, whether it is an e-mail, newsletter, video, group, network, or story. The key to marketing going viral is a simple number: 1.1

If you can get every 1 person who receives your message to pass that message to 1.1 people who also share your message with 1.1 people and so on, it will go viral. The more people that pass it along, the more exponential the growth. It's simple math.

If each person that receives the message doesn't pass it on, the idea dies off. However, if the marketing message is shared even 1.1 times for each person, that extra 0.1 makes all the difference because it means the idea will grow and be shared by more people. Then your idea goes viral. It's all in the difference of which side of the number 1 your marketing plan falls that will determine its viral success or failure. To go viral you must have an idea that people want to share.

By getting past the number 1.1 all sorts of things have gone viral, and the easiest way for them to go viral is the Internet because it's

---

so easy to share ideas by forwarding, posting, linking, retweeting, commenting, and inviting.

Having your idea or communication go viral has to be executed differently depending on the online channel such as e-mail, video, and social media and all of these channels are discussed in this book. However the concept of 1.1 is always the same. So you need to create something so compelling that people want to share it with more than one other person.

Slideshare

The Basics:

Slideshare is a business media website for sharing presentations and documents of up to 100MB. Users can upload a Microsoft Power-Point presentation, Excel spreadsheet, Word document, or Adobe PDF for viewing.[66] Presentations can also be synced with audio files to create Slidecasts, a truly virtual presentation. It has grown rapidly and claims 25 million monthly visitors.[67] What's unique about Slideshare is that its viewers can download, rate, and comment on presentations, creating a social feedback component to otherwise static presentations. This is compounded by Slideshare's presence as an embedded application on other social media sites such as LinkedIn, Facebook, Twitter. Slideshare has also created mobile capability that allows presentations to perform flawlessly on mobile devices.

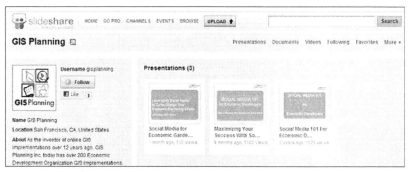

Image 17: Slideshare Page for GIS Planning.

What Economic Developers Need to Know:

One of the great values of Slideshare is how interactive it is. Users may access Slideshare presentations on an organization's Facebook or LinkedIn page, or see it embedded in a Twitter post about a relevant topic. Viewers have several ways to find the content of an EDO as well as businesses within a community. Once viewers have a presentation in front of them, they can see all the comments that other visitors have made and engage in a discussion of the ideas from the presentation. Ratings can be given, allowing useful information to be filtered. Slideshare also utilizes a tag system which will show users similar presentations to yours in a sidebar. This works vice versa as well. If you've tagged your presentation with relevant keywords such as economic development, your city, etc., viewers may see your presentation while looking at other presentations with similar keywords. Keep this in mind when you choose what keywords to enter for your presentations. Slideshare also makes it simple to get in contact with you. If a viewer sees your presentation embedded in Facebook or LinkedIn, they may contact you through those sites; however they always have the option to email directly from your presentation slides as well.

RSS

The Basics:

RSS (Really Simple Syndication) is a web syndicated format of XML (Extensible Markup Language, a type of computer code), and simply put, when content on the Internet changes, RSS uses this XML code to syndicate that new information to subscribers. When RSS is integrated into a type of online media (website, blog, video/photo sharing, podcast), individuals can subscribe to that RSS feed and receive instant updates from the source. The updates are sent to you and aggregated into a "feed aggregator" or "news feed." Google Reader is an example of a feed aggregator. The reader will connect with all those RSS feeds that you've told it to subscribe to, and stay in constant contact, grabbing new content whenever it's available, and aggregating it into a feed that you can see all in one place (inside your Google

Reader). Your reader becomes a virtual newspaper of new information and updates from the sources you select. Think of RSS as a bare bones news update feed similar to the AP or Reuters *Wire*. The one big difference being that *you* decide what news is important to you and who you want to hear from. RSS comes in three main versions that are slightly different from each other:

Version	Market Share[68]
RSS 0.91	13%
RSS 1.0	17%
RSS 2.0	67%

Figure 25: Because RSS 2.0 is by far the market leader and has the most features that EDOs use, we recommend using RSS 2.0.

What Economic Developers Need to Know:

Imagine that there's a blog that you're particularly fond of reading. The organization that produces the blog always puts out interesting content that you find valuable. You generally check the blog for new posts or updates every few days or weekly. Sometimes there is a new blog post when you check the site, and sometimes there's not. If that blog uses an RSS feed, you could sign up for it. "Signing up" for RSS simply means telling your feed aggregator, such as Google Reader, to check your favorite blog's RSS feed for new content—it never comes with SPAM or other strings attached. Below, you can see an example of an RSS feed button on Buffalo Niagara Enterprise's website.

Image 18: RSS Feed on the Buffalo Niagara Website.

Now, if you think that sounds valuable to you personally, you can assume that it will be valuable to your own audience looking to hear from you about new information from your website or blog.

RSS feeds give EDOs a fantastic opportunity to efficiently and effectively disseminate valuable information from other communication channels (website, blog, podcast, etc.) at no added cost (time or money) to a wide audience. Using RSS feeds allow EDOs to:

1.) Practice Permission Marketing—only those who choose to sign up for your RSS feed will receive your updates.

2.) Save your audience time—by accessing information through a "feed reader" or "news aggregator," your audience won't have to check every one of your communication channels to learn about new information you've added.

3.) Give your audience information in real-time—RSS feeds update in real-time, meaning your audience hears from you at the moment of publication.

Blogs

Blogs, short for "web-logs," are a powerful Web 2.0 form of communication that has empowered people to become citizen journalists. It gives bloggers online voices that many people can engage with by reading, responding, and sharing. The top blogs have over 10 million unique visitors each month,[69] making some blogs more read than many of the largest newspapers and magazines in the world.

Your EDO can implement blogs to provide your CEO, President, or Director a communication channel to be the face and voice of the organization by posting information showing his/her leadership and vision. The opinion and commentary of your organizational leader matters and can influence others' opinions.

But the blog is not, and should not be, for your top executive to communicate. The blog should be for anyone who is outward-facing to customers. Each voice ads to the richness of the organization, the quality of the information, and personality communicated. This is very different from an old model in which the only communications come from the CEO, Communication Coordinator or Marketing Director. Today, communication and marketing is a team effort as was discussed in Chapter 1.

Blogs can be short or long. They can be formal, but are typically much more informal to provide a voice and personality that is different in tone than a news release or an annual report. They are informative, opinionated, topical, and include photos, video, and links. This provides an opportunity for each staff member's personality to shine through.

If you are initially uncomfortable with the idea of having multiple members of your organization posting blogs on their own, have them submit their blogs to be approved or edited by your managers before they are posted. After the people posting and those approving the posts become more accustomed with this process and what is appropriate for a blog post, you may become more comfortable with them posting the blogs on their own.

Remember, if you trust them to make a public presentation to an elected body, a group of businesses, or investors of your organization, blogs simply require a similar level of presentation and communication skill.

Talent Attraction

Attracting an educated and skilled workforce is a critical aspect of drawing businesses to a community, and many economic development organizations are evolving their talent attraction strategies to include both the Internet and emerging social media platforms.

For example, Greater Louisville Inc. has created a Talent Attraction Forum to work closely with local human resources professionals to share ideas and best practices on how to attract skilled talent to the Greater Louisville region. Moreover, this forum is merely one component of their various talent attraction initiatives designed to help individuals considering a move to their region. Greater Louisville Inc. works in close partnership with employers, recruiters and relocation organizations within the region to provide relocating individuals with the resources they need to learn about the region and familiarize themselves with the Greater Louisville region. Other Talent Attraction initiatives include a half-day course called "Louisville 101" to rapidly immerse recently relocated employees and spouses into their new hometown, and a 12 minute "My Louisville" marketing video to showcase Louisville's character and charm. All of this information, along with links to their social media properties, is directly integrated within their website.

Image 19: Greater Louisville Inc. Talent Attraction Initiatives.

In fact, social media is increasingly becoming a vital avenue for targeting talent, creating a new form of head hunting called "social recruiting." This is particularly true with regards to targeting young professionals and the next generation of the skilled labor force. According to a recent survey by leading-edge recruiting website JobVite, 92% of those hiring in 2010 had already (or planned on) using social networks to hire employees.[70] Of these, 86% use LinkedIn, 60% use Facebook and 50% use Twitter for their recruitment efforts.

Social Recruiting: LinkedIn

With its professional focus, LinkedIn offers a wide variety of recruitment tools to find the ideal candidate. You can either take advantage of paid services such as job postings, job credits or LinkedIn's Talent Advantage, or leverage many of its free tools and resources to connect with potential job candidates. LinkedIn has many great examples of success stories on their website, highlighting how LinkedIn members have found better jobs through its network.

Case Study:

LinkedIn for Professional Development

Thinking of Linkedin's benefits only for your EDO limits its broader value to you as an economic developer. It's also for your own professional development. You can find future employment through your connections on LinkedIn and people in EDOs that are hiring will use LinkedIn to identify who they are connected to that are also connected to you. These connections serve as excellent references as they evaluate hiring you because they are much broader and less biased than just a list of referrals on a resume.

An economic developer I know was actively pursuing a new job and a key element of his strategy was to be very active on the large economic development Linkedin groups like the International Economic Development Council and the Economic Development Leadership groups. He took thoughtful effort to post useful information and respond to questions other economic developers were asking.

He shared with me that he directly credits his posts on these Linkedin groups with him getting three face-to-face interviews at an economic development conference.

To get started, it is important to connect with people you already know within your industry, who may be a great source of references or leads, or likewise whom you can help connect with the right candidate. This includes connecting with current and former co-workers, clients and partner organizations as well as participating in local and industry specific groups to establish a relationship and credibility with people outside of your network. Once you have established that network and relationship, you can post job openings not only in these network groups, but also on your LinkedIn status.

You can leverage LinkedIn's advanced search tool to define detailed parameters for the specific skills and expertise that you are seeking in a job candidate, including title, location, industries, groups, seniority levels and years of experience, to name a few. In addition, you can save this search as a Search Alert, and LinkedIn will run this search as often as on a weekly basis and automatically e-mail you the results.

Social Recruiting: Facebook

If your organization already has a Facebook page, this should be the first place to begin reaching out to your local community for people who care about the region and may want to participate actively in your organization. Providing up to date information about your organization, as well as painting a picture about the quality of life in your region, provides your local community members with a means to build a personal relationship with your organization and its goals. You can use this page to post job openings and encourage community members to spread the word to potential candidates. There are also various applications for your Facebook page that can facilitate your recruitment efforts. For example, the Work For Us application by AppBistro enables companies and organizations to post jobs and receive applications directly onto their Facebook page.

In addition to connecting with the local community in your region on a personal basis via your organization's Facebook page, one of the most effective ways to reach your target audience on Facebook is to create highly targeted ads. Given its enormous scale, Facebook provides an incredible ability to target ads, and gives you the freedom to pay per click (i.e. the number of people who clicked on your ad) or pay per impression (i.e. the number of people that are exposed to your ad).

Citysearch provides an innovative use of Facebook ads, where they recently put up an ad on Facebook that targeted only that hiring manager's Facebook friends.[71] Given Facebook users can "like" and share ads, this automatically creates a personal referral program that, at least in Citysearch's case, proved to be extremely successful.

Image 20: Citysearch's innovative recruitment ad on Facebook.

You can also search for people on Facebook by using the Facebook Directory, or post jobs directly to the Facebook Marketplace, where you can specify requirements such as location, job category and title, description, etc. Given the highly personal nature of Facebook and the fact that it includes an expanded network of friends and family (vs. just the professional focus of LinkedIn), this dramatically increases the reach of people who may be able to refer you to the talent that you are seeking.

Social Recruiting: Twitter

In addition to building a relationship and creating an on-going dialogue with your followers, you can also leverage Twitter to broadcast your search for talent. One of the best ways to get started is to connect with other local networks that are focused on sharing information about jobs within your region. There are job-related Twitter accounts for practically every region in the country, and you can easily find them using the advanced search capabilities on Twitter. If there isn't one in your region, create one yourself—or partner with local recruiting firms to create one; and then retweet their job postings to provide your followers with important information about available jobs within the region. When you have available job posts for your organization, tweet them directly to your followers, and ask them to spread the word.

You can also leverage hashtags, which are essentially keywords prefixed by a "#" symbol to help people filter for that keyword on Twitter. Common job-related keywords include #jobopening, #jobpost, #recruiting. Another trick is to leverage Twitter Search[72] to find people by location or hashtag. For example, if you are looking for research assistants or marketing staff, you may be able to search for that keyword in your region to find local people who have an expertise—or at the very least an interest—in that area.

Image 21: Regional Twitter accounts promoting local jobs.

Integrating and Distributing Social Media

With so many different social media platforms out there, it is important to find ways to maintain and manage the content you produce, both for your own sake and for the sake of people that are interested in following your activities on a professional and personal level.

One way to do this is to include your social media accounts within the signature block that you use in your email correspondence. Many professionals stick to a format that includes their name, job title, organization, and contact information in the form of phone and email. This format does not recognize the other ways that people can now interact with you. Consider adding a line or two to your email signature that encourages people to connect with you on LinkedIn and Facebook, follow you on Twitter, and join your Facebook or LinkedIn group. Below is an example:

John Doe
Executive Director
Anytown EDC
123 Fake Street, Anytown USA
555-555-1234
jdoe@anytownedc.org

connect with me:

Additionally, provide these same links on your website and enable sharing through social networks. Here are two examples of two EDO websites that do this.

Image 22: Social media links on the Nashville Area Chamber of Commerce website.

In the example above, the website provides visitors with the ability to click on the links which will take the person to the LinkedIn Profile, Facebook Page, Twitter account and so on. Once they arrive on these pages they can follow or become a fan of the EDO.

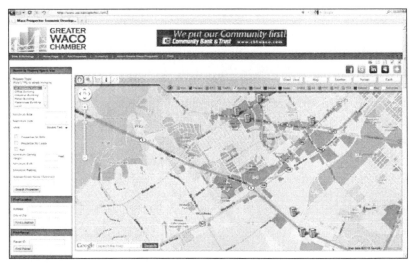

Image 23: Social media links on the Greater Waco Chamber site selection website.

In the example shown above, the organization has embedded social sharing right into the site selection process. The website visitor can take any of the property, demographic reports, or industry analysis and post links and information on their Facebook, Twitter, LinkedIn updates and more. Local residents sometimes share demographic information they are proud of and the EDO can promote featured properties directly from their GIS site selection website into their social media communications.

It may seem like a new or unusual way to promote information, data, and properties for your community; however, based on website metrics data analysis, people are already doing it.[73]

Aggregating Social Media

An effective way to promote and aggregate your various social media presences is by signing up for a Community Connection Page on ZoomProspector.com, the online network where businesses are conducting nationwide site selection searches and connecting with economic developers and site selectors. This free Community Connection Page service creates a listing page for your organization that is searchable from a directory of EDOs, and that is also visible as a link from the profile of any community that is within the service area of your EDO. You can customize the page with text, pictures, and hyperlinks to describe your community and the work of your EDO. When you list your contact information, you have the option to integrate your Facebook and LinkedIn accounts as icons within your contact information. Entering the name of your Twitter account will add a dynamic feed right on your page that will constantly update itself with your tweets. You can also include a feed from your YouTube account, which appears as a simple series of screenshots that will launch videos right on the Community Connection Page when clicked. By aggregating all of your social media content that you are already producing in one place, the Community Connection Page communicates what is happening within your community and your EDO to expanding businesses that are using the website to determine where to locate. To sign up for your Community Connection Page, visit ZoomProspector.com.

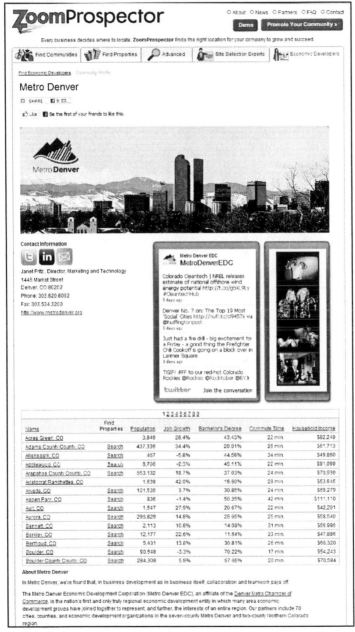

Image 24: Community Connection Page for the Metro Denver Economic Development Corporation.

Identifying and Engaging the Right Customer in Real-Time

There is a clear upside for economic developers as the possibility of social network identity portability opens up, which is that it can enable you to more effectively interact and serve your website visitors. By enabling these technologies on your websites, EDOs will be able to provide their visitors with not only an easy way to sign up and participate, but also ways to quickly judge which visitors offer the most value to the EDO's goals. For example, economic developers that have enabled this functionality on their sites will be able to tell whether visitors are business owners, site selectors, venture capitalists or talented workers, simply by viewing the profile that is associated with their login.

Real-time Location Awareness

In addition to being able to quickly qualify who is visiting your website, you will also be able to track where a visitor is when they visit your website, often down to the exact street address, via location-enabled browsers, mobile global positioning system (GPS) or self-identification of location. Also, using services such as Twitter Search, Foursquare, and Google Latitude, economic developers will be able to ascertain where certain individuals are even if they do not visit the EDO's website.

This can be extremely useful for economic development efforts, especially when a website visitor is visiting the EDO's website while at the same time physically present in a community that the EDO serves. By knowing this, savvy economic developers will be able to offer location-specific advice and possibly even offer to meet with the website visitor in person. For example, if a CEO is visiting a community for a trade show and has broadcasted his location or the fact that he/she is in town, a savvy economic developer could use that information to invite the visiting CEO to a meeting—or even just send them a list of the best local restaurants and bars near them.

It has always been possible to guess the general location of a website visitor through using web analytics tools that track IP addresses, but for the most part this is usually only accurate to the state level, whereas new technologies will provide exact street location or GPS

110

coordinates. Also, whereas it is nearly impossible to know who a user is by looking at the IP address that they visited from, new location technologies are often associated with a user's profile as we have previously discussed.

Many of these services are built to work on smartphones, such as the Apple iPhone and Google's Android phones, which are GPS enabled and allow the user to easily identify themselves and their current exact location. Further advances in both hardware and software, as well as overall user adoption, will make smartphones a major device from which people visit economic development websites, and these location-enabled devices will open up new ways for savvy economic developers to interact with their website visitors.

Seven Steps to Social Media Success

Step 1: Create a Personal Profile online

Economic developers that portray themselves as "the real me" online—i.e. use their real name, title, contact information, recent picture, etc.—instantly become more trustworthy when interacting with other Internet users, especially when it comes to commenting on blogs and posting and discussing on real-time services such as Twitter, Facebook, and LinkedIn Groups. A recent profile picture that shows people your personality and/or professionalism is key to establishing trust, as many users will get a first impression of you from your profile picture. New services such as Facebook Connect and Google Friend Connect allow you to build one central profile and then sign in or sign up using that central profile on any website that has enabled one of these services.

Step 2: Create your organization's "personality" online

In addition to creating and using a personal profile, EDOs that spend time to create and use an online "personality" for their organization will also be able to build trust and authority online. As a key driver to a community's success, EDOs can offer a variety of services to a wide range of stakeholders. After EDOs establish a recognizable online identity, these stakeholders will be able to easily follow and disseminate the organization's updates. Examples of these organizational profiles are Facebook Pages, LinkedIn Company Profiles, and ZoomProspector.com Community Connection Pages.

Step 3: Interact often and consistently

Social media is not a one-way street. Think of it more as a multidirectional street, where instead of just updating a website on a regular basis, economic developers must constantly provide updates, advice and offers while at the same time responding and interacting with concurrent online conversations. The more economic developers interact online—both with stakeholders and general Internet users—the more these stakeholders and users will turn to the economic developer for advice and updates. The snowball effect that this creates means that the more an economic developer creates value, the more people will pay attention to what the economic developer has to say.

Step 4: Monitor and respond with proof in the form of links

The real-time aspect of social media necessitates that economic developers must constantly monitor and respond to what Internet users are saying or asking about their EDO's community. New search engines such as Twitter Search that are updated instantaneously provide a tremendous opportunity for savvy economic developers to respond within minutes of a question being raised. In order to deliver the highest value when responding online, economic developers should provide a link to a URL that offers relevant, helpful, in-depth information on the topic being discussed. This is especially true when a stakeholder such as a business owner, a site selector, a local commercial real estate professional wants to know more about the economic developer's community.

Step 5: Promote and Aggregate Your Social Media Profiles

As you establish a presence on the various social media platforms, it is very important to make sure that all these different online identities form a cohesive and consistent picture of your organization and community. This is already true of your marketing messaging and collateral; you just need to apply the same principle to your presence on various social networks. The next step is to make sure to leverage that overall presence; otherwise you will miss the real value of creating these online identities in the first place. Finally, make it easy for your audience to find links to your social media profiles—for example on your website, newsletters, and even within your e-mail signature. Think of these as an extension to your business card. Furthermore, the ZoomProspector.com Community Connection Page is a great free tool to aggregate all these different online identities into one page. Not only does your Community Connection Page provide your audience with one place to follow your social media activity, but it actually gathers together much of that content right on your page, saving people the time of having to check all these properties to find out all they can about your organization and your community.

Step 6: Use location awareness

Knowing an Internet user's location and how to leverage that knowledge to offer more relevant and timely responses will be a key differentiator for success in social media. This does not mean that economic developers necessarily need to track specific stakeholders (except perhaps in certain cases, such as when a site selector is out scouting locations), but rather they need to monitor certain keywords, locations and topics that relate to their community. When someone has indicated—either through an automatic location method such as location-aware browsers, or by actively broadcasting their location—that they are in, around or planning to visit the economic developer's community, this is the time for the economic developer to provide a location-relevant response or offer. Note: As long as the user has agreed to broadcast their identity in some way, and the information that the economic developer offers is useful, in Web 3.0 this should not be construed as any kind of invasion of privacy.

Step 7: Always create value

The more you give, the more you'll get—never has this been truer on the Internet than in social media. With the majority of Internet users broadcasting self-serving or non-important information about themselves, the few people/organizations that actually offer value quickly rise to the top. Economic developers, therefore, need to always offer help without the expectation of immediate reward. As more people begin to recognize an EDO as a helpful and trusted source of local knowledge, the rewards for the local economy will start to pile up.

Engagement and Rapid Rewards

Economic developers that offer consistent engagement in an authentic and helpful manner have the ability to reach a large audience in the era of social media. People online are already carrying on discussions that could impact the vitality of an EDO's community, and economic developers that are not contributing, monitoring and responding will lose businesses and talent to other communities. With social media economic developers can build relationships in real-time online, and then deepen the relationship after trust is earned. This process is much shorter than traditional networking strategies and therefore engagement brings about rapid rewards. Overall interest in the EDO's community, new site location leads and attracting talented labor are only a few of the positive outcomes that can come about from active engagement in real-time.

E-mail & Newsletters

11

The very existence of flamethrowers proves that sometime, some-where, someone said to himself, 'you know, I want to set those people over there on fire, but I'm just not close enough to get the job done.'

—George Carlin

E-mail is an invention that allows EDOs to reach people and businesses located near or far. Often this is done in volume through the use of newsletters from your organization to educate and update people specifically interested in your community about what's new and important. However, many other people are using e-mail. In fact, 247 billion emails are sent every day. 200 billion (81%) are SPAM.[74]

It's no wonder then that several filtering gates serve to protect end users from SPAM. There are typically three main gates that your email must pass through to get to your customers' inboxes:

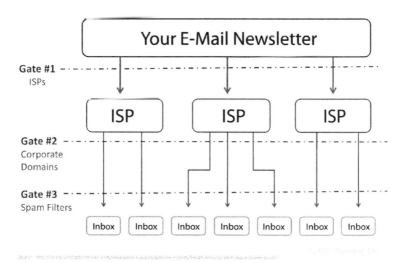

Figure 26: E-mail gateways.

The first gate is the Internet service provider (ISP) gateway. This first filter is mainly dependent on the sending IP address' reputation which is influenced by complaints, SPAM traps and high unknown user rates. The second gate, corporate domains, mainly filters email through their system administrators, who develop blacklists to keep out SPAM. The final gate is a SPAM filter. This filter mainly addresses SPAM triggers based on contents of your email.

If your email and online newsletter campaign is going to be successful, you have to make sure you avoid a few very important traps as well as maximize the value of your offering.

5 Things to Avoid:

1.) Complaints

These can come from a variety of sources such as a "report SPAM" button in a user's mail client, a manual addition to a blacklist, or a direct complaint to an ISP or system administrator. Complaint rates as low as 1% can have an impact on your email deliverability.

2.) SPAM traps

SPAM traps are addresses which are often deliberately placed on websites to tempt SPAM bots to harvest them. It's a good idea to avoid randomly placed addresses. These often show up on purchased or rented mailing lists as well.

3.) High unknown user rates

If you have many dead or unused addresses on your list, ISPs may decide not to deliver to your active addresses. Bounce rates of approximately 10% or more are susceptible.

4.) Blacklists

These come in a variety of forms. There are public and private blacklists, and you can get onto them for several of the previously mentioned reasons. It is absolutely critical that you stay off blacklists. It's a good idea to ask if you can be whitelisted by users sometimes (tells filters that your email is not SPAM).

5.) SPAM triggers

We've all received SPAM and you might have noticed that they have some common characteristics such as:

- ALL CAPS
- Exaggerated punctuation !!!!!!!
- Too good to be true phrases: "You've won 1 million dollars" or "Free trip to Mexico"

13 Things to Do:

1.) Send email only to people who have given you permission
This is the golden rule of Email Marketing. You will sacrifice early numbers for control of your reputation. This avoids interruption marketing and instead focuses on customer-centric engagement.

2.) Build your email list
Take a multi-faceted and organic approach to building your list:

- Link to opt-in forms on website/blog/social media channels to sign up
- Collect emails at local events (fishbowl of business cards)
- Share opt in forms with other organizations (Chamber of Commerce, City, etc.) with the recipient's permission
- Provide incentives to sign up

3.) Clean up your email list
Remove previously unsubscribed or bounced addresses. This helps avoid ISP blocks and blacklists.

4.) Make it easy to unsubscribe
Continue with the golden rule of permission based communication and allow your subscribers to leave if they don't find value from your emails. Not only does this drive down complaints, but federal law requires it.

5.) Optimize with social media
Cross reference your social media and newsletters so that your various communication channels are clearly available to your clients. If you're providing good solid content, people are more likely to want to subscribe to your other networks.

6.) Provide relevant content

This is pretty obvious. If you're bothering to send an email or newsletter to someone, they should want to read it, and they should learn something from it. As obvious as it sounds, many emails and newsletters are vacuous. Take some time to plan out your message and ask yourself: Would I find this interesting to read? Does this provide value?

7.) Killer subject line

Be direct, to the point and make clear the value of the contents inside.

8.) The "From" label

Leverage your brand by making it clear who the email is from. Keep this label consistent so your readers know what they're getting.

9.) Keep the most important content "above the fold"

More readers will see anything above the fold (the area of a web page seen before a user has to scroll down). Your most important information should be before this "fold line" to ensure that it's being viewed.

10.) Good mix of text/images

Use the 80/20 rule. Roughly 20% of your email should be media and 80% text. These are an accentuation of your message.

11.) Ask and respond

Remember, this is a dialogue! Just ask your readers what they want to hear about or learn. Lose your ego and find out what's important to the people who are reading your newsletters—you just might be surprised.

12.) Segment your readers

If you know you have different subsets of readers, specialize some of your content to those different segments. You can also use some monitoring metrics such as click-throughs to determine if demographics or some other segmentation is more successful with different groups. If you are targeting a bio-tech audience, don't send them an e-mail about automobile manufacturing.

13.) Test and iterate

Try A/B tests with half of your mailing list (splitting your list into two groups—A and B) and test out different subject lines, email lengths, delivery times. Track the results and make improvements from them. The key is to keep testing. Some results may or may not be related to your tests, the only way to make sure is to keep testing and improving.

Story:

"Max Growth" SPAM

Before one of our clients was our client, I learned about their organization through an e-mail in my spam folder. I sometimes scan through my spam folder to see if anything important gets inadvertently sent there by the spam filter. The e-mail and the marketing campaign was titled "Prescription for Growth" and it followed by saying "For Max Growth—Move Your Company to (community name deleted in this book)." It seems like a pretty straight-forward marketing campaign because they were specifically targeting pharmaceutical companies. But there was one big problem with this campaign that they didn't consider because they are good economic developers and not spammers. They didn't think about how spam filters would evaluate their e-mail.

If you are like me and get hundreds of spam e-mails each day, you also get e-mails that promise "Max Growth." Think about it… think about it… OK, now you remember the e-mails I'm talking about.

So this quality EDO sent out a legitimate e-mail campaign to a targeted audience of pharmaceutical companies and the spam filters assumed it was spam offering prescription drugs for max growth. It just goes to show that no good e-mail deed goes unpunished.

Connecting Businesses to your Communities

12

It was clear by the late 1990s that the Internet would meaningfully transform corporate site selection analysis, but that there were very high hurdles to overcome before this could become reality. Chief among these obstacles was gathering a critical mass of EDOs to create a meaningful platform for efficient online site selection. Also, at that time, there were many information and technology barriers preventing the effective implementation of a quality system for the process on a large scale. An especially vexing challenge was how to connect the right businesses with the right communities.

Story:

Making a National Site Selection Decision System

GIS Planning had already built a few dozen community and regional GIS-powered site selection analysis websites for EDOs by the late 1990s. We were helping a lot of EDOs maximize the opportunity to grow and attract companies by enabling businesses to prove to themselves why our clients' communities were ideal business investment locations based on hard-facts, reliable data, and geographic advantage.[75]

We thought a necessary, complimentary online service would be to provide a nationwide site selection portal that could aggregate data for every community across the country so that any business could go to one website to connect with EDOs. We had the idea for this back then and wanted to build it. But the problem with this model was that it required data from across the nation and we only had a few dozen clients in a few states, so our breakthrough website would have to wait. Trying to launch a national site selection website at that time wouldn't have been credible and would have been as useless as starting a national hotel reservation website that only included hotels in a few cities.

Over the next few years our clients grew exponentially and before long we had clients in the majority of the states. We correctly projected that our growth would continue, with our technology being implemented in 30 to possibly 40 states in the (then) near future. We were confident that our client base was about to hit a critical mass of national relevance, so we started building our national site selection website called ZoomProspector.com.

Our aspirations grew as we waited for it to become a possibility. We wanted it to be more than an aggregation of data from our clients, so we decided we would build a national site selection website that included searchable data for *every* city, county, metro, and state in the nation.

Our passion has always been for small and medium sized businesses because they are the core of our nation's economic and job growth. Yet they are the most disadvantaged when it comes to accessing quality data and business intelligence because they can't afford expensive consultants and don't have analysts on staff to figure out the best geographic locations to succeed. You just don't find site selection analysts on the staff at the local ice cream parlor. But no matter how good their product or service is, choosing the wrong location for the business could cause them to fail.

Our mission was to empower all of the 750,000 businesses each year that start-up or expand to a new location[76] by giving them site selection tools, no matter their size, revenue, or sophistication.

We also focused on the many small and medium-sized communities because most businesses are unfamiliar with their locations. Everyone knows New York City, Los Angeles, and Chicago, but they may have never heard of Ponca City, Oklahoma even though it, like thousands of other places across the nation, could be ideal for their business to succeed.

There are millions of businesses and thousands of communities that could be a perfect match for each other if they could find each other. The businesses are looking for communities that can provide the right employees, revenue growth, access to markets, and business mix. The communities are looking for companies that can provide new jobs for residents, tax revenue for city hall, and customers for existing businesses. But the businesses and communities couldn't find each other because of an information barrier of not being able to find and be found. The Internet could change all that. So we designed ZoomProspector.com to be a matchmaking website to break down the information barriers and act as a search tool to match businesses with communities based on the site selection criteria that mattered to the company. (For those that read the story on page 6 about online dating, you now realize why matchmaking matters in economic development and for ZoomProspector.com)

In the spring of 2008 we launched an invitation-only private beta of ZoomProspector.com at the Web 2.0 Expo in San Francisco, the largest and most successful Internet conference in the world. One of the reasons that we did this was because we wanted to show people in the Internet industry that there was significant online innovation coming out of the economic development profession. Also, we wanted to size up our web technology with the very best in the world because all of the best companies were there.

We actually had three ways we launched the website that day. First was the news announcement, then a demo booth at the expo, and finally a launch party.

To give you an idea of just how much the media had changed from our first product launch to this one, the news broke about our first product launch in 1998 in *The Wall Street Journal*. We chose to break the story of ZoomProspector.com in *TechCrunch*, the second most read blog in the world, because we thought it was a more important audience to reach than we would get through traditional business media.

During the exhibit hall booth demos, we met with numerous power players in online technology. There were many demos but one that stands out in my mind was an unusually long demo (usually you need to show a demo in a couple of minutes) to Steve Chen, the co-founder of YouTube. He kept listening and waiting for me to show him more about the website, so I did. He said, "I like it. This is great."

Image 25: Anatalio Ubalde presenting to Steve Chen, co-founder of YouTube and Peter Chu, co-founder and CTO of TradeVibes.

I always wondered if economic development was too obscure for anyone to know what we do, but I can assure you all that even among the tech digeratti they get what we do and think it's both important and cool.

We threw a big launch party that night in a hip venue in the trendy South of Market neighborhood. It attracted nearly as many people as the Yahoo! and IBM parties which were near ours.[77] And aside from one of our staff at the door initially telling Tim O'Reilly (the Web 2.0 Expo is his conference) and Clay Shirky (the keynote speaker that day and a new friend I met at a private event the evening before) they couldn't come in because they weren't on the guest list, the party went great and the product was well received.

About five months later, after making improvements based on feedback from the beta period, we launched the website publicly at the Hard Rock Café during the International Economic Development Council conference—where a full quarter of the conference attendees showed up. Since then, economic developers have

Image 26: At the ZoomProspector.com launch party with Clay Shirky (author of "Here Comes Everybody") and Tim O'Reilly.

been excited about how this technology helps their communities get discovered by businesses. You can see photos and videos of these events on YouTube and the ZoomProspector.com website.

The website has been successful since its public launch in October of 2008. It has experienced strong usage and has been embraced by both companies and the business media. ZoomProspector.com has been featured in the most respected traditional and new business media including *Forbes, Fortune, Bloomberg BusinessWeek, Inc., Entrepreneur, TechCrunch*, and *Mashable. Inc.* magazine described ZoomProspector as a step in the evolution of the site selection process: "Legendary retailers Sam Walton [of Wal-Mart]and Ray Kroc [of McDonald's] used to hunt for real estate at 30,000 feet; they used private planes to survey the country for prime spots in which to open new stores. Now a new website, ZoomProspector, attempts to provide business owners a similar bird's-eye view of the commercial landscape from their desk chairs."

The New York Times says in its article, "The Basics of Starting a Business," that "Along with doing Google searches, you should also check out trade publications and association Web sites. If your business is in retail, look at ZoomProspector, which provides helpful information on local economic trends (population, income and demographics). Visit Yelp.com and see how many competing retail outlets you'll be facing. Is the market too crowded?" We are happy to be listed with Google and Yelp as one of the three resources businesses should use online to evaluate their market.

Since the launch, many of the traditional business media companies have relied on ZoomProspector.com analysis and data to evaluate the best locations for companies, start-ups, and small businesses in articles they have published. Today, EDOs serving over 13,000 cities across the nation are directly participating in ZoomProspector.com, and the website provides data about every city in the nation to businesses looking for a new home.

Image 27: ZoomProspector.com

Choosing a Domain, Sub-Website, or Microsite

13

A mong the big issues you have to decide on when creating your website is its domain name and where it lives. We'll assume that you already have a website and it already has a domain name.

However, if your website isn't producing the results you want or delivering the traffic you expect, it may be because your organization is lost within a larger website, or perhaps one website is not enough for your goals and initiatives.

When You're Lost in a Bigger Website

Many EDOs exist as a department or division within a larger entity such as a local government or Chamber of Commerce. Especially within a government website it's easy for the ED division to get hidden among dozens of other departments, especially all of the ones with more staff and bigger budgets. But this may also occur in a Chamber organization that is primarily focused on traditional member services.

In these cases you may want to consider creating your own website which visitors can link to from the "parent" website. Making the right decision depends a great deal on your situation and goals.

Here are seven things to consider when deciding what will work best in your situation:

1.) Do you have information you want to update frequently and are dependent on someone outside of economic development to update for you? If that answer is yes and that outside person is slow to meet your needs, you probably need your own website.

2.) Can you achieve your specific communication, traffic, transactional, and strategic goals within the website of the larger parent entity such as the city/county or Chamber website? Your audience and needs are often very different from a general government department audience.

3.) How easily can a visitor get from the home page of the parent website to your economic development pages? Will the design of the overall website cause visitors to your economic development pages to become lost or misdirected to non-economic development pages?

4.) If the "parent" website is uncommitted to improving, does being associated with the parent website reflect negatively on your economic development organization's image? I've seen many municipal website that are terrible and would reflect poorly to a company considering making a business investment in the community.

5.) How large is the area you serve? Often, the smaller the city the more often it can operate under a parent website.

6.) Does your potential website have a highly targeted audience, even more so than a general economic development website audience? Targeted and micro-marketing are growing areas of marketing and that can be seen in the emergence of micro-websites.

7.) What would you as a customer want? This issue is central to the success of your website.

Tip:

How Government EDOs Can Demand More Visibility on the Home Page

Too often government websites are organized like city hall's organizational chart. This may make sense for the City Manager or Human Resources Department, but it doesn't make sense to your website visitor.

There are basically four types of visitors to a local government website: residents, businesses, visitors, and children. If one of the four audiences is business, then the website should have a link to your department's website. This is a solution that focuses on how to best get the customers to the government services they want the fastest.

Microsites

Although it used to be popular to have just one website, a new trend that many companies and economic developers are following is the development of microsites. These niche websites help the organization tailor its information and message to a tightly-focused audience, sometimes as specific as one individual company or industry. This allows the organization to provide focused, relevant information that doesn't get obscured under the umbrella of the larger EDO website. The danger is even larger if the economic development is a division under a larger organization such as a Chamber of Commerce or government website.

The old way of thinking that your one website should be the only destination no longer works as an operational model, because although it remains interconnected, your Internet presence is distributed now. Important destinations for your EDO to be found no longer exist just on the public web, especially due to social media.

This now liberates you to become a multi-website-location organization that hyper-targets communication and marketing to specialized audiences through direct website addresses. One-to-one marketing was always the promise of the Internet and microsites are a reflection of that strategy.

There are a growing number of economic development microsites that are independent and successful. These include microsites for EDOs targeting specific industries such as a bio-tech, land and buildings GIS analysis, and even company-specific websites. Most have their own website addresses and can be linked to from the main EDO website, while others may have the option to be either independent or embedded within the parent website. For example:

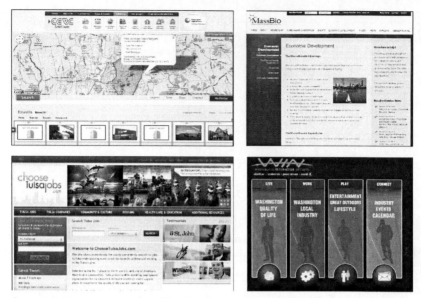

Image 28: Microsite examples of the Connecticut Economic Resource Center's Site Finder, Massachusetts Biotechnology Council for economic development, Choose Tulsa Jobs, and Washington Interactive Network.

Hiring the Right Website Developers & Internet Strategists

14

Imagine how quickly you would fail if you decided that all aspects of marketing and communications for your EDO could all be done by a single consultant. In this predestined disaster your logo designer would design your corporate communications strategy, your website developer would define your competitive positioning, your video producer would plan your social media strategy, and your public relations firm would tell you which industries to target. All of this would be done by one consultant, effectively putting all of your eggs in one basket.

It sounds ridiculous, right? That's because it is. You wouldn't do this for your traditional marketing and communications, and you shouldn't do it for your online strategy. Now, your online strategy incorporates all of the traditional elements of marketing and communication. On the following page, Figures 27 and 28 demonstrate the old way of marketing and communication, and the new way.

Marketing & Communications (Old Way)

Advertising
Brochures
Site selection information
Meeting Businesses
Direct Mail
Familiarization Tours
Special Events
Newsletters
E-mail
Media & Public Relations
Telemarketing
Website
Videos (VHS or DVD)
Press Releases
Trade Shows

Figure 27: In the old way of viewing marketing and communications, there were many different strategies, and online strategies were just website and e-mail.

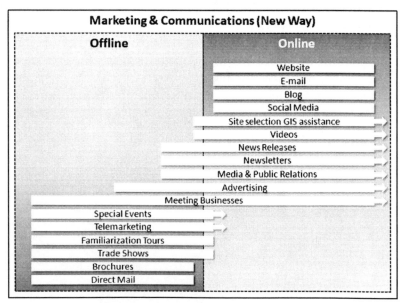

Figure 28: The New Way of marketing and communication.

In the new way of viewing marketing and communications, nearly all strategies are online and encompass many of the traditional offline strategies. Today, nearly all effective marketing channels have some online component. Even traditional face-to-face activities, like trade shows, include booths with large computer monitors connected to the EDO's website; telemarketing can be automated, managed, and measured using online tools; and special events are being streamed live over the Internet. Now communications are moving online leaving only a few of the traditional marketing methods offline, like brochures and direct mail.

The Internet has become increasingly diverse and broader in scope, tools, channels, and complexity. There was a time when having a static HTML page was all you needed, but that was more than fifteen years ago. Now there are many elements of a successful economic development online program, including your website, video, social media, GIS site selection, microsites, distributed apps, news releases, blogs, web conferences, e-mail, SEO, analytics, and more. The Internet has become so specialized that any consultant who tells you they can do it all for you is full of it. If they claim to be the master of all Internet trades, they are the master of none. You need real experts that are the master of their unique piece of the Internet.

Website development, GIS site selection, social media, e-mail communication, positioning, public relations, and each of the other elements of an effective online strategy are different skill-sets. You need the best people with the best skill-sets working on each of your online strategies.

The new reality of marketing and communications for your EDO is that you, the economic developer, must coordinate and be the center of your online initiatives—and you should be! This is a fundamental shift in how economic development professionals must see themselves. Your online presence and strategy needs to be directed by you and implemented by multiple expert consultants, your own staff, and all of your outside partners and community ambassadors. You or your Marketing Director is now the coach that directs all of the players' activity, but is not responsible for actually doing all of the implementation. The vision and coordination of your efforts is too important to outsource to someone outside of your organization like a consultant that doesn't intimately understand the day-to-day issues, values, and opportunities of your organization and business community. You can't say, "Don't worry, our website developer is taking care of our online strategy," unless you want to fail. You are the leader in representing your organization and the Internet is the most comprehensive way to do it. So if you want great results, you must lead and take charge.

How to Hire the Right Website Developers and Internet Strategists

Tips for hiring the right website development consultants (or staff, if you are a large organization):

Tip 1: You Need a Deep Team

You will need to hire multiple vendors with excellent skills in their specific online expertise. The Internet is too specialized for any one company to do everything well. If a company says they can do it all, you can eliminate them from consideration. Someone who does a lot of things pretty well is called a handyman and you don't want a handyman building your website.

Tip 2: Positioning First, Hiring a Website Developer Second

One of the issues that EDOs often think about when creating their website is that they want a website that makes them unique, and so they incorrectly rely on their website developer to accomplish this. This confuses and combines two issues that should be separated (and I'll explain shortly why companies that call themselves economic development website developers want you to be confused about this). First, you can have a unique website, but that won't make your organization unique. What makes your organization unique is your story—your competitive advantage for businesses. You may already know what your story is, or you may have hired a highly qualified consulting firm with experience marketing places to help you craft your story. The story is your differentiator and your website is where you tell the story. The story comes first and the website comes after. You are much better off hiring a first-rate marketing company to craft the story of why your location is a special place to do business than have a website developer creating your story when they are building your website.

Yet companies that call themselves economic development website experts pitch that they will create the best website in the nation for an EDO. They claim that it will be unique because not only will they build the website, but they will help position the EDO's unique story. These vendors primarily do this so they can obtain a larger amount of money from you. Because they are confusing the issues, it sounds reasonable. But don't be fooled—you need to have your positioning story first, and after you do, you can look for a website developer to present your community's story in your website.

In the early days of the Internet, your website was your Internet strategy. You could go to one vendor to handle all of your online needs because there was only one need—your website. EDOs, and the website developers serving EDOs, understood this relationship. But the Internet has changed so much since then, and your website is just one element of an effective online strategy today. EDOs got in the habit of working with just one vendor to solve all their online issues. Those vendors loved that because it meant more and more revenue for them. Even now they are trying to keep all of the revenue for themselves by misleading EDOs that they are a one-stop shop for all things Web, when they are mostly just website developers.

Tip 3: Selecting What is Standard vs. What is Unique

When EDOs write down what they want their website to be, it's very common that they say they want it to be different and unique without actually explaining what that means.

During the process of defining what you want for your website, an issue to consider is what parts of your website you want to be standard and unique. A reasonable knee-jerk response would be "we want everything to be unique," however you actually want a combination of standard and unique elements.

While you want distinctive imagery and design on your website to distinguish the feel of your website, you should not feel the need to redesign every last piece of functionality on your website. For instance, you will notice that there are standard methods found on websites for how a user replies to a blog post. The reason they are standard is because they work well, and users are now accustomed to how that feature operates from all the other websites they visit. If you try too hard to put your unique stamp on this feature, or on other tools common to most websites, you run the risk of confusing your audience while in pursuit of the "wow" factor.

Although your EDO may want to have a website that is unlike any other EDO's website, consider your motivation for wanting that. If it is to stand out to provide a great user-experience, information, and the best available tools to serve businesses and site section professionals—that makes sense. But if you want to be different just so you are different, then you may be reinventing the wheel. There are best-practices that your peers are already implementing and by modeling these features and tools for your own EDO, you can benefit. Many of these best practices are covered in this book. Additionally, by using standard tools, services, and features you reduce your costs.

Ironically, some companies that call themselves economic development website developers promise you uniqueness, but these websites are often only different visually. The reason for this is the vendor has a standard development template for creating all of its websites with the same tools for all of their clients. By having a standardized platform of features it's cheaper, faster, and easier for them to crank out websites to all of their customers that have the same internal guts (content management system and features) but a different skin (graphic design). It looks different, but really isn't.

Remember, your main goal is not to have a website that is different from everyone else's, but a website that is better than everyone else's. Rembrandt didn't reinvent the paintbrush; he simply used the standard tools available to him to create content that surpassed his peers and "wowed" everyone. You can do the same. That being said, we are big supporters of innovation on the Internet, so if you believe you have come up with a breakthrough idea of a new feature, selection, or tool on your website, then go for it. Even if it isn't a major innovation, if there is something that is special to your organization, find a way to include that to show your uniqueness on your website. But always remember that your focus is to create the best website you can.

Tip 4: Hiring a Website Developer

There are plenty of good website developers out there. There is no need to pay a lot for a standard website, even if it includes things like a blog, social media integration, video, etc. These are standard features. Don't get sold that you need to pay specialty prices, even if the consultant claims to be an expert in economic development websites. With the strategies in this book, you can create a great economic development website with the website developer of your choice on a reasonable budget and hire national experts when you need them.

Website developers have different skills that they bring to building your website. When evaluating a potential vendor you should consider the experience, team members, value, price, how the website will be maintained, if you want a local or national vendor, ability to deliver on time, and project management method, just to name a few of the considerations. Because you will want other specialized tools for your website and you are likely to hire other outside experts, identify if a prospective website developer has worked collaboratively with other Internet strategy companies, integrated other vendors' website tools (blogs, GIS, social media feeds, etc.), and are comfortable taking direction from the firm that developed your marketing/positioning strategy (such as a destination marketing expert).

So many website development companies come and go that it's challenging to keep track of them, but if your EDO is going through the process and would like feedback about your finalists or a vendor you are considering hiring, feel free to contact us for our input and recommendations. We can most likely give you rapid feedback because we know a number of website developers that are good, and others you may want to avoid.

Tip 5: Your Website Tells a Story

As was just mentioned, a key element of your website is the story it tells, and that story must be developed before the website is constructed. It's a mistake to assume that only people who work as Internet strategists or developers can tell your story. What you really need is someone who is an expert in marketing places and economic development organizations—someone that knows how to help your organization craft its unique story. These experts tend to include traditional marketing, destination/place marketing, communications, and public relations firms. Once they have helped you develop the story they will also be able to work with your Internet consultants on how to tell that same story through your website, social media, video, e-mail, and other efforts. Because this is the case, offline experts can be very valuable for your online strategy.

Tip 6: Implementing the Right GIS Tool

Chapter 7 covers some of the key elements of a successful GIS website for economic development. However, for identifying the best GIS tool for your EDO you may also want to consider how being a client of the vendor expands your long-term benefits and expands your access to additional online visibility. One of the things I have professionally focused on is the value that EDOs can receive by connecting their websites, social media, and GIS tools into strategic online networks that are much larger. For example, there is significant benefit by having the properties on your GIS site selection website integrated and marketed through a national website portal that is an established corporate real estate site selection destination, and which is co-promoted by highly respected corporate real estate media publications. These types of integrated and distributed marketing relationships provide your EDO with high value because they expand your ability to be discovered by businesses through established site selection website destinations.[78]

Also remember that, like your website, your GIS tools are long-term investments that will need to be upgraded over time as technology improves. When hiring a GIS site selection analysis website developer, you should consider the vendor's ability to meaningfully invest in research and development. The vendor must constantly innovate by building the best technology available in order for your organization to be successful.

Tip 7: You Aren't Building Just One Website Anymore

There are many different online platforms, channels, and networks. Your website is a central online strategy, but it can't be the only one. Think of your website as a node in orbit with other online nodes that connect to each other. These other nodes include, but are not limited to: microsites, social media platforms, site selection portals, partner websites, news, push-and-pull communications, and search engines.

Hire the very best expert for each strategy you choose. They will know how to implement the web strategies with each other under your overall control. If they don't know how to coordinate their activities into your overall strategy, then they certainly aren't the best and you shouldn't hire them. Your consultants must be able to network together, integrate when appropriate, and understand this new world of online economic development, one in which we increasingly live in an Internet-centric platform for all marketing and communications.

Search Engine Optimization   **15**

Your brand isn't what you say it is. It's what Google says it is.
—Chris Anderson, Wired Magazine Editor-in-Chief

The Basics:

Search engine optimization (SEO) is the art of improving your website's relevance and importance (the two ways search engines classify websites in accordance with search queries) on the Internet. Many people confuse SEO with search engine marketing (SEM)—a term that generally involves paid search engine advertising—or liken it to attempts to "game the system" and stuff keywords in the underbelly of a website to trick search engines into ranking it higher. Good SEO is fundamentally not an attempt to game the system. Matt Cutts, one of Google's most long-standing SEO employees, pointed out that Google is perfectly happy to have organizations and individuals attempt to optimize their site for Google. According to him, optimizing your site simply provides Google with the most context-sensitive and informative data about your website.[79]

SEO can seem overwhelming, but the reality is that its core principal is extremely simple: produce quality content. The absolute most important factor in search engine optimization is something you should already be doing anyway—providing valuable content to your audience. You can try every single trick in the book, but if you don't have good content, no amount of "optimization" will save you.

According to SEO experts at SEOmoz,[80] Figure 29 explains the most important features of good SEO from the bottom up. The foundation is good, quality content that is easily "readable" by search engine spiders, robots or crawlers. These automated bots roam the web reading content so that it can be stored and indexed against search queries extremely quickly. To help web crawlers read your site, make sure that important headers, titles and keywords in your page are in text format. Having too many of these important web page elements in graphic format (if you are using images, make sure that they have text attributes embedded inside their HTML code), animation (such as Flash), or scripts (Javascript) can stop a web crawler from seeing content inside your website. Having a site map on your website can also help web crawlers find their way through your website. Next on the pyramid is keyword research and targeting. You should take some time to develop keywords for your website that you feel best describe your organization and the way your audience describes the services you offer. Backlinks are also an important concept in SEO. Backlinks are essentially inbound links to your website from other sites. Because another site has linked to yours, they in effect vouch, or vote, for the quality and content of your site. It's very important to understand that having a large quantity of backlinks is great, but that links from sites that are older and more authoritative are ideal. If you can get your website or blog linked from a well-respected website, other sites are likely to start following suit—so focus your efforts on being linked to other great websites rather than finding a huge number of links from mediocre sites. Also keep in mind that having one of your keywords ("economic development" for example) as the anchor text (the portion of a hyperlink that you see and click on a web page) of an incoming link to your site is much better than something generic like "click here." Finally, the top portion of the pyramid is small for the moment, but growing rapidly. Social media is coming onto the SEO scene as more and more social networking sites start to integrate with search. Facebook has an agreement with Microsoft Bing, Twitter is searchable from TwitterSearch and all of these are likely to see more mainstream search integration in the future. The best way to prepare your organization for this piece of SEO is to create a social media presence for your organization (see Chapter 10).

SEO Pyramid

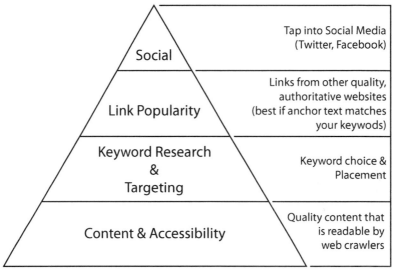

Figure 29

What Economic Developers Need to Know:

SEO is a constantly changing field and to be successful in it, you'll have to monitor and change your keyword strategies as the market dictates (see our additional resources to for help). However, these *12 Recommendations for Economic Development Keywords* are an excellent starting point for EDOs:

1.) The name of your organization
The most obvious keyword is the official name of your organization (however, it's possible that some businesses' only contact with you may be through your website, so your URL (uniform resource locator—web address) is also a good keyword choice

2.) Variations on your name
There may be some slight variations on your official name, such as "Anycity" Economic Development Corporation, "Anycity" EDC, City of "Anycity," or "Anycity" City

3.) Misspellings of your organization

This may come as a surprise, but misspellings can be critical keywords. Plenty of users misspell words in their searches and having common misspellings can help your ranking (e.g. Pittsburgh, Pittsburg, Pitsburg, Pittsberg, Connecticut, Conneticut, Connetticut). Note that you should not put the misspellings in your website. They should be used as keywords in your online advertising or SEM.

4.) Add "economic development"

Simply adding "economic development" to some of your other keywords is a good strategy (e.g. "Any city/county/region" + economic development)

5.) Geography + Demographics

EDOs often have some of the best demographic information and make it more understandable than websites like the US Census. Apply some of those categories as keywords (e.g. Population, Income, Demographics, Education, Labor).

6.) Geography + Specialty or Focus

Add specialties or particular expertise to your geography keywords:

"Your geography" +

- Site Selection
- Foreign Direct Investment
- Business Expansion
- Business Relocation
- Entrepreneurship
- Incentives

7.) Your geography's name + map/maps

In addition, consider geographic elements that are map-related:

- Minneapolis map
- Boise maps
- St. Louis interstate
- Detroit downtown
- Houston office park

8.) Your geography's name + GIS or geographic information system
Power users, site selection consultants, corporate real-estate professionals, and analysts are searching directly for these high-value website tools.

9.) Your geography's name + property
All variations of property types and terms can be keywords (e.g. industrial, office, research/office/business park, shovel-ready, certified site, retail, shopping center, mall, strip center).

10.) Your geography's name + business
Rather than "economic development," users may just be thinking about "business" (e.g. Spokane business, Rochester businesses, Anchorage Industry). Major business names in your area are also good keywords (e.g. Kodak Rochester, Dell Roundrock, Wal-mart Bentonville).

11.) Your geography + business assistance
e.g. Saginaw business assistance, Charlotte small business service, Waco entrepreneurs, Pensacola how to start a business, invest in Rhode Island, Minnesota incentives

12.) Your geography + major industry
e.g. Austin software, Houston energy, San Diego bio-tech, Salinas agriculture

Most of these recommendations highlight the growing trend of users implementing more specific and tailored search queries. Figure 30 shows that in the last two years alone, the number of words per search phrase has grown, meaning that users are becoming more specific about what they search for.

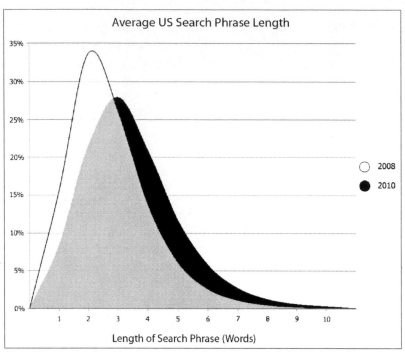

Methodology: Data is collected from Uptrends.com's web analytics service called OneStat.com. All numbers mentioned in the research are averages. Research is based on a sample of 2 million visitors divided into 20,000 visitors of 100 countries each day.

Figure 30

After you've developed a solid list of keywords, you've got to decide where to actually put the keywords so that they can start working for you. Make sure that you use keywords naturally and authentically in your content. You won't be doing yourself any favors by making your content look unnatural.

When integrating keywords in these places, follow these recommendations:

In your Website

Use keywords in page titles, appropriate headers, body text, and URL links, but make sure not to stuff pages with multiple mentions of the same keywords—this actually lowers your ranking.

In your Property GIS

Having as much data as possible is a good strategy when it comes to your GIS web application pages. Try to have geographic identifiers with your data and organize your properties by type with details and sub-categories (e.g. office park, call center, flex). One thing to stay away from is linking out to third-party demographic or business data vendors. This transfers some of your SEO clout from your page to the third-party sites (you are essentially voting for them over your own page in some respects).

In your Blog

Follow similar rules to websites: write naturally and for your readers—not the search engines. Make a special effort to fit keywords into the titles of your blog posts and where it's appropriate, mention your keywords in the body of your post.

In your Social Media

Shorter is better in social media (Twitter only allows 140 characters) Utilize things like #hashtags in Twitter (see pg. 105 for definition) and be concise. Remember that you are representing your organization, so while it's fine to be friendly and personable (in fact it's preferred), only comment or post on professional subject matters (not about the errands you ran that day). Content is king in social media just as it is in your website and blog—if you don't have something relevant to add value to a conversation, don't post or comment.

In your News Releases

News releases are more powerful than press releases because they live forever on the Internet and anyone can get to them. Include keywords in your news release titles and body when appropriate. Using a professional service will usually provide you more value because other established news websites often take feeds of these news release services' announcements and put the same content on their websites, further distributing your news on the Internet.

In other websites

Posting on other websites (such as the comments section of another blog or social media such as LinkedIn) is also possible thanks to Web 2.0. If you have something valuable to post, weave your geography and some of your keywords into your post if it makes sense for the topic of discussion. Remember, you're a guest on other websites, so practice good etiquette and never post anything that could be considered spam or out of context self-promotion.

Google Instant

At the time of the writing of this book, Google released *Google Instant*. This new search feature alters SERP (search engine results page) pages real-time based on every letter that a user types, and as a result, has the ability to change what being on the "1st page of Google" means. It is also significant for online advertising and keyword selection (longer, more specific keywords may not be as valuable as they once were if Google starts showing several SERP pages before a user has even typed one single word). It's not clear exactly what Google Instant will mean for SEO or online advertising, but you should take note of such a development.

Online Advertising

16

Google has become the remote control for the world; it's the first stop, not TV.

—Will Margiloff, CEO of Innovation Interactive (Denstu)

The Basics:

Online advertising offers a significant competitive advantage over offline advertising in a variety of ways. In the early days of the Internet, it offered lower transaction costs than traditional offline advertising. The infinite "shelf space" of the Internet meant that digitally, your ads could be simultaneously everywhere at once, no longer inhibited by geography or time.

As the Internet has continued to grow in size—both in terms of number of users and the amount of data that can be transferred via high-speed broadband connections—online advertising has opened up an even greater competitive advantage over older media formats such as print advertising and television (for more on broadband's impact, see pg. 15).

Some advertisers shied away from the Internet early on because it didn't create the same emotional experience that television offered. Today, however, online video (Hulu, Netflix, YouTube, Vimeo, Newscasts) and audio (iTunes, Pandora Internet Radio, Podcasts) are dominating users' time and growing rapidly. High-speed Internet has allowed online advertising to cut deeply into the market share of television and print media with few signs of letting up. Although many critics panned the viability of online advertising after the dot-com crash which started in 2001, the advertising channel has evolved and grown to more than three times the spending during the height of the dot-com bubble.

**Internet advertising revenue growth
1999-2009**

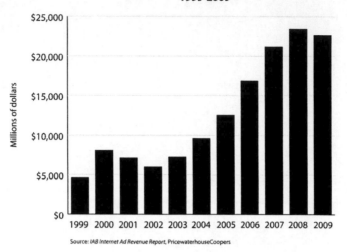

Source: *IAB Internet Ad Revenue Report*, PricewaterhouseCoopers

Figure 31: The Internet has seen strong revenue gains in the last decade.

2009 U.S. cross media advertising marketshare

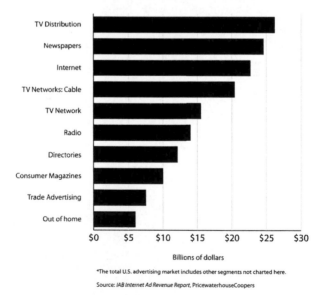

Billions of dollars

*The total U.S. advertising market includes other segments not charted here.

Source: *IAB Internet Ad Revenue Report*, PricewaterhouseCoopers

Figure 32: Internet is catching up with TV for marketshare.

What Economic Developers Need to Know:

Since businesses are performing research and finding answers on the Internet, it is where your organization needs to appear at the *Moment of Relevance* when businesses are making decisions. This should be accomplished through a variety of channels. Showing up in search results is especially valuable. Because search connects someone at the very moment they are looking for something, it offers the lowest cost per customer acquisition according to research by Piper Jaffray.[81] Online search is about half the cost of Yellow Pages, and less than one-fifth the cost of online ad displays, e-mail, and direct mail.

There are typically two ways you can show up in search results. One is organically, and we provide you with Search Engine Optimization (SEO) recommendations in Chapter 15 on how to get ranked through your online content and keywords. The second is through paid search, which is sometimes referred to as Search Engine Marketing (SEM) or Search Engine Advertising. Paid SEM usually consists of three different models of online advertising strategy: Performance-based, Impression-based, and a hybrid of the two.

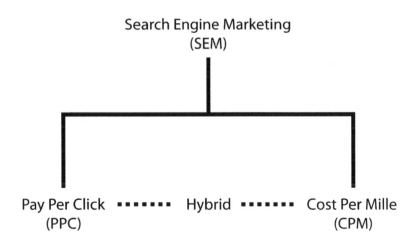

Figure 33: Search Engine Marketing tree.

The PPC (Price Per Click) model, sometimes referred to as a CPC (Cost Per Click), is an example of performance-based pricing. Performance-based pricing is so named because no fee is charged for your advertisement unless your ad is actually engaged (clicked-on). Performance-based pricing stands in opposition to the more traditional interruption advertising strategy of CPM (Cost Per Mille), which is an impression-based fee that charges an advertiser for every 1,000 (mille) impressions displayed online, regardless of whether anyone clicks on the ad.

In the past several years, performance-based advertising has gained in popularity, and in 2006 it surpassed the more traditional impression-based model. Hybrid systems have declined along with CPM as more advertisers are converting to a strictly performance-based pricing model.

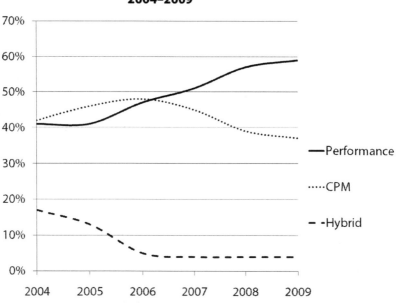

Source: *IAB Internet Advertising Revenue Report*, PriceWaterhouseCoopers

Figure 34: Performance-based pricing is the new king of online advertising.

Performance-based models are enticing to organizations of all sizes, but they are particularly useful to smaller organizations or businesses with limited advertising budgets (there is no minimum budget requirement for Google's AdWords). Because you are only charged when an ad is clicked on, your investment is protected from catastrophic losses. If you're spending money using performance-based advertising, you can be sure that your advertisements are being clicked on.

EDOs' opinions about online advertising are changing; its perceived effectiveness increased 39% from 2008 to 2010.[82] 17% of EDOs planned to increase online advertising spending in 2010.[83] Yet in 2008, EDOs only allocated 1% of their budget to the tactic; and in 2010, only 21% indicated that they had increased their spending on online advertising over the past year.

Search engines continue to become smarter and add depth and nuance to relevancy search. On top of that, social media looks poised to start offering search functions that rely on referrals and recommendations from friends and like-minded cohorts. That means that in addition to the social media strategies we highlight (Chapter 10), the best combination for making your organization significant on the Internet is a combination of SEO and SEM. When a SERP comes up after a search query, the main column (shown below surrounded by a solid black box) includes information that you cannot directly affect through SEM, but can optimize through SEO to achieve better positioning organically. According to Google, these results make up about 85%–90% of total search clickthroughs. By incorporating PPC advertising strategies, you can affect the remaining 10%–15% of clickthroughs using the area surrounded by dotted-lines. These are sponsored links, or advertisements that Google places through its AdWords program.

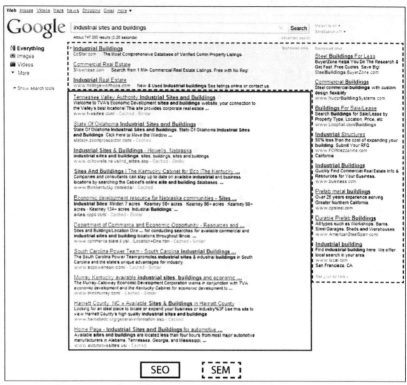

Image 29: Organic search results next to paid search results in a Google SERP (search engine results page).

Google AdWords is a PPC system that combines two sorting mechanisms to decide which advertisements show up where on Google search pages. The first is a bid system where users submit the maximum price that they are willing to pay for someone to click on their advertisement (Cost Per Click). You will never pay more than this amount per click and you will probably pay less (your Cost Per Click is actually determined by the next lowest bidder behind you). This price is then influenced by a Google "Quality" score which is determined by Google. The most important criterion is clickthrough rate. This is the ratio of users who click on an advertisement divided by the amount of times the ad is displayed. If someone clicked on an advertisement every single time it displayed, the clickthrough rate would be 1.00. Google puts a heavy reliance on the statistics of millions of people—the higher the clickthrough rate, the better an advertisement is positioned in search results. Relevance is the next most important category. Because Google's search engine is so good at determining relevance, it extends this to advertisements and matches relevant ads (based on their keywords) with search queries. The final component is landing pages. A good landing page is genuine in its intent (per the advertisement) and allows users to easily navigate to find the service or item in question. It should also have very few (preferably zero) pop-ups. Landing pages that follow these guidelines will not be penalized via the Quality score. Landing pages shouldn't be an issue for your organization if your website is well organized.

For help getting started with Google AdWords, you can find tutorials and informative videos at:

EconomicDevelopmentOnline.com

Web Analytics

17

The Basics:

Collecting data about your website

The Internet provides one of the most data rich environments we have ever known. Launching a great website and social media campaign is an investment, and like any good investment, it should have measurable outcomes to help track and make sense of that investment. You can't manage what you can't measure and without good metrics, you're shooting completely in the dark. Data matters and we have entered an era where enormous databases and statistical analysis make intuition by itself a risky endeavor.[84] This point cannot be overstated. Those who choose not to measure their performance will *always* underperform their competitors (who are monitoring and analyzing their data) in the long run, and economic development organizations have a responsibility not to let that happen if within their means. The good news is that there are many free tools available, such as Google Analytics, that make the upfront costs of monitoring very low.[85]

What Economic Developers Need to Know:

Google Analytics

Google Analytics is a free tool that places a small script inside your website that monitors many variables about the traffic to your site. It includes more than just the number of "hits" (how many users visit your website) that older sites used to measure with page counters. Google Analytics variables are diverse: bounce rate (how often someone leaves your site immediately after arriving), the location of users viewing your website, the average amount of time spent on your site, the percent of new users to your site, how many users were referred to your site from other sites, and many, many more.

Image 30: The Google Analytics Dashboard—your gateway to the numbers behind your website.

Google explains: "Google Analytics shows you how people found your site, how they explored it, and how you can enhance their visitor experience."[86]

When collecting data that is so rich and has so many options, it's very important to make the distinction between meaningful metrics and analysis and simply collecting data. Google Analytics will provide you with countless data, but that data provides very little value by itself. All economic development organizations should absolutely be monitoring their websites and social media; however, setting out a proper strategy for what to do with that data once it's collected is infinitely more valuable and will bring more significant results to your organization. That's why it's so important to start with a monitoring and analytics strategy before you start collecting data.

Making a plan

This is probably the number one most overlooked aspect of online analytics. An organization that haphazardly collects data and uses that data to make important decisions is more dangerous to itself than an organization not collecting data at all. Data and statistics bring a sense of certainty, and if you aren't looking at the right metrics within the proper context, big investment dollars can be misallocated under the guise of "data backed decisions."

When measuring what's important to your organization, a high signal to noise ratio is essential—hone in on the data that matters, and cut the noise (the rest) out. No two organizations are alike, and therefore they don't all need the same data (or it will take on different levels of importance). Setting up your plan of attack will help you filter out data that's not as useful to your organization.

The following list, heavily influenced by analytics guru Avinash Kaushik's *Web Analytics 2.0*,[87] includes several important considerations when creating your analytics plan of attack:

1.) Who's your audience?
This should be your first step. Who are we targeting? Who do we care about? Spend a lot of time on this step, and segment your audience if they are a large group. Your data may show that you're wildly influential with 13-year-old video gamers, for example. That data may feel like a pat on the back—"we must be doing something right, users love us!" But if those users can't invest in your services and you use that data to make key decisions, your ROI will suffer.

2.) What should we be measuring?
Use step one to help you think about what particular metrics are most important to measure for your particular audience. Does your organization really want new subscribers to an e-mail newsletter? If so, invest in tracking conversion rates associated with the portion of your website where users sign up for that newsletter. Your metrics should be based on your goals, don't just measure everything.

3.) Quantitative + Qualitative

Don't get stuck only looking at the numbers. Yes they can be big and far reaching, yes they can be impressive, but often numbers only tell you *what* rather than *why*. It's very easy to make the wrong assumption about why your numbers look the way they do. Spend some time probing qualitatively why you might be getting the numbers you're looking at. Simply ask your clients. There are numerous free tools to help you do this such as 4Q.[88] Surveying your customers and asking them what they want is one of the easiest ways to optimize your site. Reach out to users through social media and engage them about what they want to see improved or offered. This step will also help you formulate some of your goals (i.e. your customers' complaints or suggestions can help drive the goals for change your organization seeks).

4.) Have a hypothesis, and use it to improve your site

Once you've decided who your audience is (who to measure) and decided what metric is best for your goals (what to measure), use #3 and your organization's own intuition and expertise to formulate a hypothesis about what results might be realized from changes to your site. This will help you to create meaningful analytics tests and filter your data by things that really matter (don't just test changing a button color for the sake of analytics, think about changing a key part of the site that you think affects your goals, e.g. conversion rate). Analytics and testing can quickly become "interesting" from a curiosity perspective, leaving you looking at many fascinating data relationships, but make sure you keep your goals set and test your biggest priorities first. Having a hypothesis means you always know your success measurement (did the hypothesis—e.g., increasing the number of graphics on our website's landing page will increase our conversion rate by 15%—succeed or fail?). In the example given, it's clear that the conversion rate and graphics are what we're really interested in. Other things may be learned from the data, but the data and testing was designed for those specific metrics and outcomes. If the results of one test make you curious about something else, great! Construct a second test using appropriate goals and a new hypothesis.

5.) Take a varied approach

Don't get stuck looking at one metric. There are many tools and metrics available, don't use them just to use them (that will add unnecessary complexity to your monitoring program), but realize that no one metric or monitoring program does it all. Set out your goals, and then go look for the tools to accomplish them. Following these steps plus a free tool such as Google Analytics can provide a huge improvement to your site. Don't buy or outsource expensive analytics until you've taken a good look at what you need—you may be able to do in-house analytics with very low costs.

6.) Don't get comfortable!

The beauty of the web is that we can get real-time data at a near constant rate. That is also a recipe for complacency. Things change very fast online, and if you aren't vigilant, you'll miss things. TEST CONSTANTLY. Just because something was true last year doesn't mean it's still true or going to be true in two months. Always expect possible changes and be ready to accept alternative causes for differences in your data. The good news is that you can test out new hypotheses straight away at little cost. Feel like something has changed in one of your target segments? Test it! As long as your sample numbers are big enough, you can use this heuristic to tell straight away if a change you made to your website was for the better or worse.

A/B & Multivariate Testing

As mentioned, one way to optimize your website is to use testing. This can be done economically by using some of Google's website optimization services.[89] Testing is easy to start and is integrated right into Google Analytics.

A/B Testing

A/B testing is the simplest way to test and is a great place to start your testing program. It's fast, cheap, and effective at getting your organization in-step with your website. An A/B test works like this:

A short script from Google is placed inside your web page and 50% of your viewers are randomly shown one variation of your web page (the A variant), and 50% are randomly shown the alternative web page (the B variant). These variant pages can be as similar or different as you want, but A/B testing works best on big changes to important parts of your page. Then as viewers visit your site, Google analyzes all of the traffic and then reports the results back to you. Once you have a statistically significant amount of website traffic (Google Analytics will alert you as to whether enough visitors have come to your site to make the results statistically significant), you can see the results.

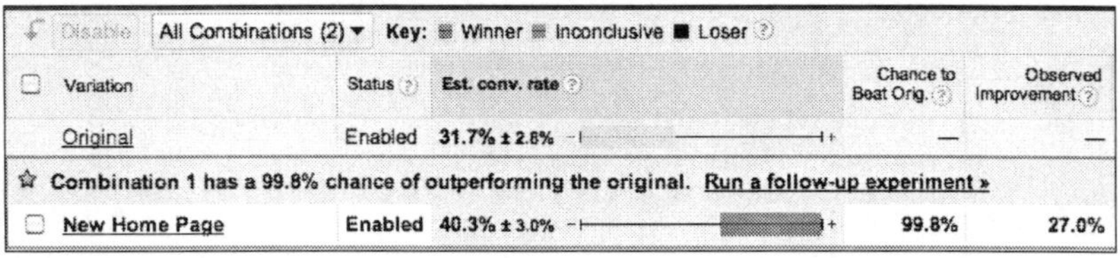

Image 31: In the above test example, the revised home page increased the website's conversion rate by 9%, showing a 27% improvement and a 99.8% chance to beat the original home page.

An important note about A/B testing:

You may say to yourself, "Why don't we just monitor our page for two weeks, collect the data, make a change, monitor the data for another two weeks, and compare the data?" This line of thought runs into a basic problem associated with sequential testing. Because experiments function better against a constant, it's important to keep all other things besides your changes as equal as possible. Imagine a website that sells children's toys, many of which are imported from China. Imagine during your second week of testing one of your changes (a change to a graphic, for example), a story hits the news about contaminated children's toys imported from China. Then toy sales slump. Any change you see in your sales and data can no longer be disassociated from the tainted products from China. You have no idea whether your sales dropped solely because of the bad news from China, because of your graphic, or some combination of both or neither. We avoid this problem by practicing simultaneous testing. The script in your website tells it to show different users different examples of your site at random within the same timeframe. Doing so makes other outside factors equal and allows you to focus on your changes when looking at the data.

Multivariate Testing

Multivariate testing excels where A/B testing comes up short. A/B testing can always test individual changes to websites, but it can never measure the way changes interact with each other. Perhaps users overwhelmingly clicked on a button when it was orange rather than blue, but when the background was black, they rejected the orange and went for the blue. A/B testing is not sophisticated enough to pick up these nuances.

Think of multivariate testing as a matrix of options, with all possible combinations considered:

Background Color	Logo	Button Color	Advertisements	Free T-shirt Offer
Black	Image	Orange	Images	Image
White	Text	Blue	Text	Text
Gray	Flash	Read	Flash	Flash
Patterned Image	None	Green	None	None

Figure 35

In Figure 35, we have five different factors, at four levels (or differences methods). This means that 1,024 possible combinations are available (4^5). Google Website Optimizer utilizes a full-factorial method of multivariate testing, meaning that all possible combinations are fully tested (other partial-factorial testing exists, which tests fewer combinations, but uses those interactions to infer other results). You can immediately see how powerful the potential of this type of testing can be. By the end of your test, you'll know which one combination out of 1,024 different interactions yields the best results for a particular target action you specify (signing up for a newsletter, for example). It's important to note that there are drawbacks to multivariate testing. Full-factorial testing can take a very long time depending on how much traffic your site receives. If, for example, to be statistically significant, 100 samples of every targeted action are necessary (again, let's say you choose to use newsletter sign-ups), 102,400 viewers of your website must subscribe to your newsletter before your test will yield meaningful results. If your website doesn't see that kind of traffic, an A/B test is probably a better solution. One excellent strategy is to start with A/B testing, find out what big changes work best for your site, and then use multivariate testing to test smaller changes to optimize your big change. For more information about testing, including video tutorials and testing strategies, please visit:

EconomicDevelopmentOnline.com

Working on the Web 18

Give a person a fish and you feed them for a day; teach that person to use the Internet and they won't bother you for weeks.

—Author Unknown

Recent changes in Internet technologies and heightened expectations of EDOs have caused them to explore the use of new Internet tools to leverage the Internet not just for marketing, site selection, and communication, but also for what can be considered core operational infrastructure and functions for EDOs.

General to Specialized

Economic development staff's technological infrastructure is usually tied to the larger organizations with which they are established, such as local governments or Chambers of Commerce. Yet many of the core functions of economic development did not necessarily fit into the molds of their parent organizations. They were challenging to implement using general desktop software intended for business use, or specialized governmental applications that didn't satisfy EDOs' needs. As a result, economic developers would often resort to using generic database and information systems such as ACT, Goldmine, Microsoft Excel and Access, or FileMakerPro for core functions, tracking and management.

To fill the needs that are more specific to EDOs, a few specialized programs have been developed by economic development focused companies. Two options are ExecutivePulse, Inc.'s eponymous ExecutivePulse, and Blane Canada Ltd.'s Synchronist. Primarily intended to serve the Business Retention and Expansion needs of EDOs, both of these applications have added a few additional features in attempting to meet the growing needs of EDOs.

Living in the Cloud

A more recent trend for both businesses in general and EDOs in particular, is a move to cloud computing, also known as Software as a Service (SaaS). Cloud computing offers several advantages to the older models of software because both the applications themselves and their associated data live on the Internet. This gives organizations investing in cloud computing the ability to securely access data from any place connected to the Internet and to collaborate more effectively. Cloud computing also lowers entry costs and provides features to organizations that would generally not be able to afford a traditional "standalone" software package.

Many readers may not recognize it, but when you access your Gmail, Yahoo Mail, Hotmail, or other email accounts online via a web browser, you are using cloud computing or SaaS. The same convenience that consumers expect from their personal email has been extended to business systems.

In the next decade, Cloud Computing is likely to take on an even stronger role in our activities. According to the Pew Research Center, 71% of 371 technology experts[90] agreed with the following statement:

> By 2020, most people won't do their work with software running on a general-purpose PC. Instead, they will work in Internet-based applications such as Google Docs, and in applications run from smartphones. Aspiring application developers will develop for smartphone vendors and companies that provide Internet-based applications, because most innovative work will be done in that domain, instead of designing applications that run on a PC operating system.[91]

Desktop computing isn't likely to disappear for some time, but its role is going to be diminished by the affordability and versatility of the Cloud.

Online Documents and Applications

Already there are online office suites such as Box.net and Zoho that feature traditional Microsoft Office Suite authoring applications like word processing, spreadsheets, etc., but go further to incorporate additional features such as collaboration, project management, case management, time tracking, and more. A major reason that companies are investing in these online services is that, unlike traditional software packages which feature a new version every three or so years, online applications are updated more frequently, featuring gradual, iterative enhancements that keep the users of these products up-to-date with the tools necessary to their success.

Online Platforms

Recently two global companies, Google and Salesforce.com, the originator of the Software-as-a-Service concept, have gone beyond just online office suites. They are focusing instead on creating online, ubiquitous platforms so that their users are no longer limited to just basic office suite functionality and the additional features that the companies develop themselves, because these platforms are open to third-party developers.

Google Apps and the Google Apps Marketplace

Google, via their Google Apps platform, is providing their standard email, calendaring, and collaboration tools that individuals use for free to organizations for low or even no cost, while enabling the controls over data access that businesses require. However, if the standard features of Google Apps do not meet all of the organization's business needs, Google has created, within the Google Apps Marketplace, the ability to find independently developed programs that can be added to the organization's Google Apps. For example, if an organization wanted project management tools, there are many that are low cost or even free such as Manymoon or Insightly, allowing Google Apps users to try different options to meet their business needs and select the one that works best for them.

Salesforce.com CRM and Force.com Platform

The originator of the SaaS model is San Francisco headquartered Salesforce.com. Though Salesforce.com started out primarily as a CRM (Customer Relation Management) application, it has grown more sophisticated—introducing additional features used by many Fortune 500 companies, but at the same time still scaling for smaller organizations.

Salesforce.com is designed specifically to provide the basic customer relationship management functionality of managing data, tracking activity, and quantifying results that EDOs need, but with the added advantage of being platform independent. This platform independence allows users to securely access their information from any web browser, smart phone, or other Internet-enabled device.

Salesforce.com also features a robust security platform which allows for multiple levels of sharing with EDOs and economic development partners, to enhance collaboration while maintaining the secrecy of protected information.

As the originator of the Software-as-a-Service model, Salesforce.com provides a large exchange for third party features called the app exchange. In the app exchange, EDOs will find several applications which can extend their existing Salesforce.com subscription to accomplish many tasks such as quantifiable email marketing, project management and more.

Perhaps the greatest benefit of Salesforce.com is that it is designed to be customized easily through intuitive online tools by the EDOs themselves to match organizational workflow, decision-making processes, and methods. However, if even greater customization is desired, there is a large ecosystem of Salesforce.com related companies that provide one-on-one customization to streamline an EDO's Salesforce.com implementation.

Using a Salesforce.com application built by Arc Collaborative, the Waco Chamber of Commerce is improving internal communication while quantifying and focusing their economic development efforts, in the same way a sales manager for a traditional company would likely focus on the prospects bringing the greatest value to the company.

Salesforce.com for Free

Salesforce.com's mission is to use the company's resources, people and products to improve the communities in which they live and work. The key product suite, revolving around an Internet-based

CRM system, helps businesses, nonprofit organizations, and government organizations save time and money through tracking and managing critical information in the cloud. These tools allow for greater collaboration, transparency, speed to results, and significantly lower costs across the board.

—Suzanne DiBianca, Executive Director and co-founder of the Salesforce.com Foundation, September 1, 2010

For organizations wishing to implement Salesforce.com, the Salesforce.com Foundation is the integrated philanthropy arm of Salesforce.com that offers 1% donations of time, products, and equity to non-profits.

If your EDO is a not-for-profit, you can receive free donations of up to 10 licenses, and discounts on additional licenses through the Salesforce.com Foundation.

Distributed Online Presence   19

If the hill will not come to Mahomet, Mahomet will go to the hill.

—Essays of Francis Bacon

A traditional approach to the Internet would be that businesses would find your online presence on your website. However a broader way to reach customers is to be found wherever they are on the Internet. This is a concept in which a piece of your Internet presence is distributed throughout multiple websites that are relevant to your audience. This strategy has merit because it is customer-centered versus your-organization-centered. You start your relationship with the business by bringing your organization closer to the customer instead of requiring the customer to come to you.

Most distributed strategies occur through the use of "widgets" (sometimes called "gadgets"), which are typically embeddable, small-sized web applications (often called "apps"). You've seen these before on many websites. They come in the form of updates on the current weather, breaking news, Twitter feeds, or a Google search bar to search the website you're on. Each of these widgets provides some information to the website visitor and a link back to the website of the company that offers the widget. So each distributed application is an opportunity to develop a relationship with a possible customer by linking them back to the widget developer's website.

There are few examples of EDOs implementing distributed web applications, but some cutting-edge organizations have implemented this strategy, one that will continue to grow in the future.

We saw this trend early and its new potential for reaching a growing customer audience, so we built the first distributed web applications and widgets for economic development—first for clients and now as free apps for any EDO. For the State of Pennsylvania, we built widgets that enabled the state to take demographic data reports from a site selection website we developed for them and embed the reports seamlessly into any of the other pages of its website. This enabled Pennsylvania to place detailed demographic reports on any of its webpages describing the cities and counties in its state, and across multiple website properties the state and its partners control.

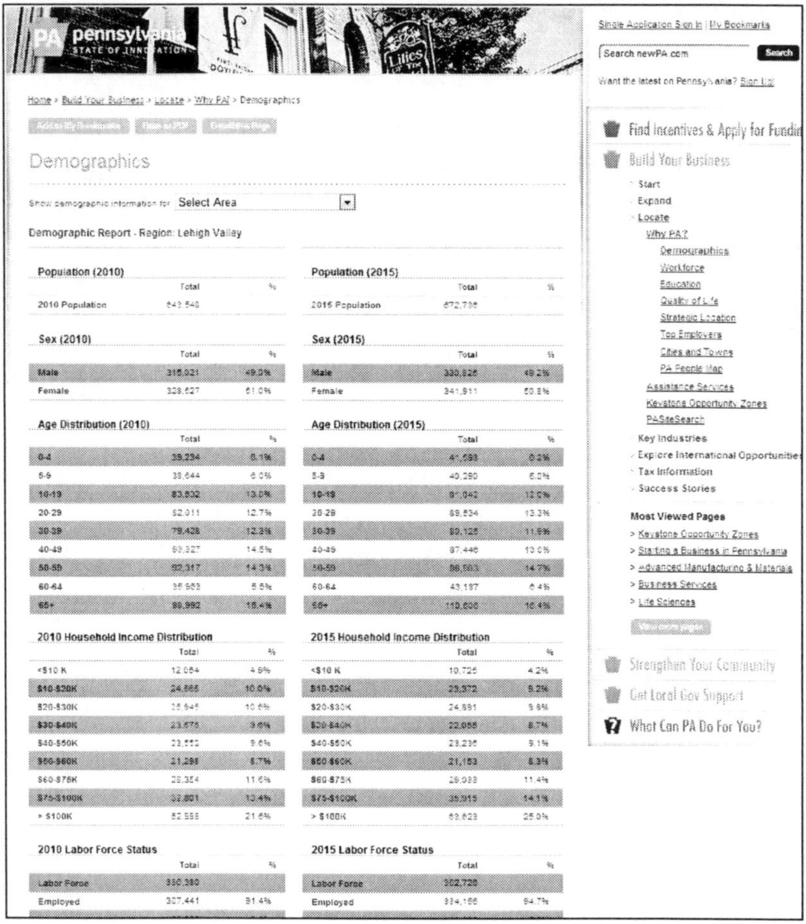

Image 32: The demographics show up on this State of Pennsylvania's economic development website with seamless integration. The data is actually showing up as a widget embedded within the website and produced by the State's GIS website system.

In Indiana, another of our state clients, we offered a widget to all of the local EDOs within the state to embed a GIS-based site selection tool on their local websites that took information from the statewide website we built. This enables the local EDO to have its own GIS site selection analysis tool on its website so that businesses can only search for properties in its service area. It also promotes the statewide organization through a hyperlink located within the widget.

Based on this early success helping our clients with distributed web applications and widgets, we built a new app that every local EDO can use to promote their communities. Leveraging the strategy of putting EDOs directly at the sites where potential customers are already surfing, we built a free Facebook app, because Facebook is now the number one online destination. Now you can install the ZoomProspector Facebook app on your Facebook Page to promote the demographics or available properties in your community. For help doing this, see Chapter 10.

The Mobile Internet

20

The Basics:

The average mobile phone is used 70% of the time for normal telephone activities like making and receiving calls, but the average iPhone is used only 45% of the time for such activities.[92] Smart Phones (iPhone, Blackberry, Android) and increasing infrastructure for network capacity from telecoms have drastically changed usage patterns for mobile devices. Even the nomenclature is changing. Instead of cell phones, we now have Smart Phones and "mobile devices" primarily because we aren't just using our "phones" as telephones anymore. According to Cisco, that demand is fueling projections that global mobile data traffic will increase by 39 times (4,000%) from 2009 to 2014.[93]

As Figure 36 shows on the follow page, the use of non-voice data applications has grown significantly over the last year:

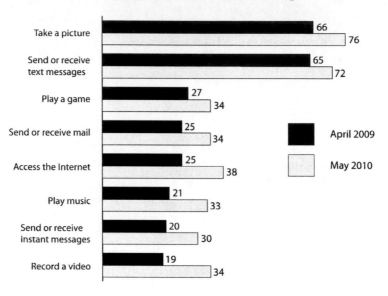

The percent of mobile phone owners who use their phones do the following

Source: *Pew Internet & American Life Project*

Figure 36

Additionally, the May 2010 Pew Center study included some new categories regarding mobile phone owners' activities:[94]

- 23% have accessed a social networking site using their phone
- 20% have used their phone to watch a video
- 15% have posted a photo or video online
- 11% have purchased a product using their phone
- 10% have used their mobile phone to access a status update service such as Twitter

The frequency with which users are accessing these activities is also increasing:

Date	Percentage using Internet on a mobile phone several times a day
April 2009	24%
September 2009	37%
May 2010	43%

Source: Pew Research Center's Internet & American Life Project

Figure 37: Frequent daily mobile Internet usage is becoming the norm.

Mary Meeker, prominent Internet analyst since 1995 and dubbed "Queen of the Net" by *Barron's*, believes that we are currently in the midst of the fifth major technology cycle of the past half-century. In her Morgan Stanley *Mobile Internet Report*, she declares: "Rapid ramp of mobile Internet usage will be a boon to consumers and some companies will likely win big (potentially very big) while many will wonder what just happened."[95]

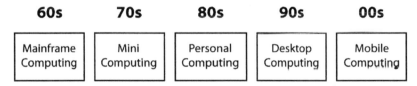

Figure 38: The five major technology cycles in computing.

Meeker points out in her report that mobile Internet technology is being adopted at a faster rate than desktop Internet technology was in the 90s. Her analysis means that mobile Internet computing is poised to ramp up much faster than we may be anticipating. Japan is a global leader in mobile technology, and the Morgan Stanley report notes the claims of NTT DoCoMo, one of the largest Japanese telecom providers, that over 90% of their service is non-voice/data. Unsurprisingly, Japan is also trending heavily towards mobile social media usage. The social networking site Mixi only reported 17% of its page views from mobile devices in 2006, but by 2009 that number had increased to 72%. The rest of the developed world is now entering the same phase of mobile Internet adoption that Japan entered from 2000–2004, and there's strong evidence to suggest that North America will follow in Japan's footsteps.

What Economic Developers Need to Know:

One key area of the mobile Internet that EDOs can start to immediately tap into is location based services. Location based services are any services that take advantage of the GPS location of a mobile device, and therefore its owner. Services such as Foursquare, Yelp, and Facebook Places are all examples of location based services.

Foursquare

Foursquare is a location based service that leverages gaming mechanics to get users to "check-in" to various businesses via their mobile devices. Once a user is inside an establishment, their check-in is tallied and their selected friends are informed. Given the sensitivity of this location-based data, services like Foursquare are extremely vigilant about allowing users to share this data either publically or only with friends that they have explicitly invited into their network. The person with the most check-ins at a particular establishment can then become "Mayor" of that establishment. This creates a competitive gaming atmosphere among friends and presents businesses with a fantastic opportunity to run specials for check-ins and prizes for mayors. Another way to think of this from a business' perspective is that a mayor is essentially that business's most loyal customer, and Foursquare has enabled businesses to not only access that data, but also to reward these loyal customers for their patronage. For instance, a business could have a new weekly prize for the mayor or any benefit they choose.

Yelp

Yelp functions both as a Web 2.0 social site that might help you find an auto mechanic or tailor in your region, or help a user on the go (via Yelp's mobile applications) find nearby basic services such as restaurants, banks, and pharmacies. Not only can users quickly locate these services on a map, but they can also see reviews and comments that other users have left regarding the businesses they find. Yelp has helped numerous businesses "get on the map" for online users who seek others' recommendations for the businesses with the top reviews. More than 38 million people visited Yelp in the month of August 2010, exploring over 12 million local reviews.[96]

At a recent technology conference that we attended,[97] the CEO of Yelp, Jeremy Stoppelman, and the VP of Product Management at Google, John Hanke, discussed the future of the Local Web. According to Stoppelman, Yelp is about connecting people who are searching for something local with merchants providing local services. For merchants, this provides a golden opportunity to advertise organically and based on word of mouth, thus moving away from the model of buying advertising and hoping for the best. Economic developers can leverage this trend by encouraging all businesses within their region to get on Yelp, who in turn should encourage their own customers to rate and review them.

Facebook Places

Facebook has recently launched its own location service called Facebook Places. While it's still relatively new, the possibilities for Facebook are vast. Facebook has over 500 million users, rich amounts of consumer data, and a model that enables recommendations/referrals from friends (Facebook "Likes")—all of which could eventually be used to point users to events/establishments where they might find value. Facebook could potentially start helping businesses find users whose given interests or friends' referrals highlight what sorts of mobile coupons or special offers (sent as credit to a mobile phone) might be recommended to an individual. Facebook could send recommendations to its users ahead of time, or as a user enters an event or business with tailored offers from their mobile devices.

The biggest strength of location based services is that they can deliver enhanced rewards to businesses' most loyal and valuable customers. Once someone walks through the door, they could have mobile coupons transferred to their mobile device, available for use only while they are in the store at that time. The user's time is tracked by how long they are inside the business and cuts off once they leave.

This technology offers businesses the ability to charge customers no more or less than the time they spend on their service as well as reduce some overhead costs. Economic development organizations could start using this technology for themselves, but more importantly, they could make sure that their local businesses are leveraging this emerging trend. Consumers are already rating, commenting, and checking-in to businesses and events all over the country; but if businesses aren't aware of it, they won't be able to access their customers' feedback (through ratings and comments), or take advantage of the incentives they could offer to their most valuable customers by simply recognizing them as important (either through cash prizes, discounts, or via basic social recognition—you are the Mayor of Business X). It's important to keep in mind that as with most things in technology, if your business doesn't provide these incentives, then customers who are early adopters will simply move on to businesses that do.

Tip:

Location Based Services and Privacy

As we mentioned in the social media section, you should always be vigilant about privacy issues regarding any of your activities online. This is just as true of real-life interactions as it is of email security and important folders on your computer or mobile device. GPS location based services are no different, and we recommend that you carefully select your preferences and options concerning data sharing and privacy for any of these services. If you are not sure which setting is best suited to your needs, always start with a conservative approach and experiment with different settings. That being said, stonewalling online services based on undefined privacy fears will hurt both your organization and local businesses' ability to connect with clients and customers and their needs. Your clients and customers are going to use these services whether you do or not. If you have privacy concerns, take some time to define and justify those concerns clearly and reasonably. Then apply any appropriate data security to those concerns while still taking advantage of these powerful services. Otherwise, you risk being left behind—wondering what happened while your competitors keep up with your target audience's evolving behavior.

Moving Forward

This book was not written just so you could learn about the Internet trends in economic development. It was written for you to take action.

As an economic developer, it would be irresponsible for you to not take advantage of one of the greatest changes that has happened in your entire career. The Internet has made it possible for you to be successful in ways that were previously unimaginable.

You can reach the world (Chapter 2). You can promote your community by teaching instead of annoying (pg. 20). You can enable businesses to convince themselves to choose you instead of you trying to convince them (Chapter 7). You can appear like a super hero just when someone is in need of help (pg. 20).

That's right; we wrote this book so you could become an economic development super hero online.

The problem with following

Geoffrey Moore's book *Crossing the Chasm* outlines the marketing of high tech products during the early startup period.[98] It focuses on the phases when customers buy a product during its adoption lifecycle, as shown in Figure 39, where the size of each phase is proportional to the number of customers. The basic concept is that innovators and early adopters are the first groups to try and use high tech products. After these small groups have used and tested the technology, resulting in acceptable benefits, large numbers in the early majority start to adopt the technology. The late majority is the next to adopt the technology as they realize that everyone is already using the technology, so they better use it too. Finally, there are the laggards, who may never be convinced. If you want an example of a laggard today, these are the people that are still saying, "I'm not sure if e-mail is going to catch on enough that I need to use it."

Technology Adoption Curve

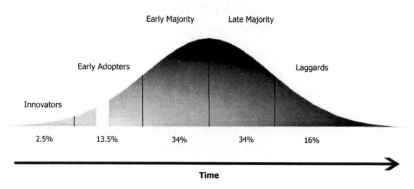

Figure 39

Even though economic developers don't sell high tech products, they are users of high tech products and services. So it is important for you to understand where your EDO exists on the adoption lifecycle. New Internet technologies come out all the time and you need to decide if you are going to try them out and use them early or wait until they have been proven effective by other EDOs.

It might seem like a much safer strategy to wait and see what works and how other people have succeeded using a technology, but it's not safe at all. It's really dangerous because you get no meaningful advantage by being a follower.

The value curve does not follow the adoption curve. The benefit goes to those who leverage the technology before everyone else is using it, because it gives your EDO a competitive advantage to be faster, smarter, more effective, more convincing, or better connected. Whatever cost savings you get from waiting for the technology to be older won't be offset by the fact that people in other EDOs are already long-time experts in the technology—they have a head start implementing it, and you are stuck playing catch-up.

The peak of the competitive value curve occurs much earlier than the peak of adoption. If you want to maximize your competitive position for economic development online, you need to move quickly to invest in and adopt new and effective technologies.

An Economic Development Quiz

During the longer national trainings I give to economic developers I ask them two questions that I will ask you now.[99] I ask them to raise their hands to give their answers but all you have to do is answer truthfully to yourself.

How would you rate your current economic development efforts online?

A. Bad
B. Average
C. Good
D. Very Good
E. The Very Best

How would you like your economic development efforts online to be?

A. Bad
B. Average
C. Good
D. Very Good
E. The Very Best

Now, select your answers and remember them. Seriously, do this.

OK, now that you've answered the questions, let's move on. The answer for the first question is simply a benchmark of where you are today. Many people raise their hands saying that their online efforts are "Bad," "Average," or "Good". Maybe that's what you chose too.

The more important answer is your response to the second question. For the second question, if you answered "The Very Best,"— good for you. But during my trainings very few people ever give that answer.

No one ever raises their hands for "Bad" and "Average". Some raise them for "Good".

The overwhelming majority raises their hands for "Very Good," and they feel very good about their answers. Maybe that's what you chose too.

But there's a big problem with "very good". I like math a lot, but it doesn't take an advanced degree in mathematics to understand the problem with "very good". No one says they want to be bad or average, a few people want to be good or best, and the overwhelming majority want to be very good. If you add up all of these answers and then divide by the number of people in the survey, you will find that the middle answer is "very good". So essentially very good is actually average. Re-read that if you need to and let it sink in.

When you and thousands of other people woke up this morning, you probably didn't go to work and say "I think I'll produce average work today." Instead you went in and did a very good job, just like everyone else.

Your EDO is not going to stand out or have a competitive advantage if all you do is very good economic development online, because so will everyone else. So you'll be average.

If you really want to be better than everyone else you're going to need to move from being very good to being the very best. OK, maybe you won't be *the* best, but maybe you will. And if you have to settle for being in the top 5%, that's pretty fantastic too.

We didn't write this book for you to be average. We wrote it for you to be amazing. Go be amazing.

Acknowledgments

Books, like economic development, are team efforts. We are very thankful to all of the people who helped make this book possible. At GIS Planning we thank Pablo Monzon for his support of this book as it again took significant staff time away from their day-to-day activities. We appreciate your support and belief that this would not only make our team smarter, but also the entire profession. Additional thanks go to Arti Kuthiala and Eric Simundza who provided tremendous research, writing, and editing support.

Outside of our company we appreciate the contributions and early feedback provided by Chad Catacchio, Judy McKinney Cherry, JoAnn Crary, Janet Fritz, Dr. Jan Jannink, Andy Levine, April Mason Nichols, Dylan Tokar, Ryan Shell, and Mario Ubalde.

Our deep thanks go to the family of GIS Planning clients who have shown us the very best in our profession through their passion and vision. They are an unstoppable movement of innovators and early adopters of Internet technology that see value and opportunity with clarity.

Acknowledgements from Anatalio Ubalde

Thank you to all of the economic developers who have shared your stories and friendship with me as I have traveled all over the planet. I've enjoyed sharing the possibilities the Internet can bring to our profession and learned a lot from you. You helped write this book through over a decade of sharing and feedback.

Thank you to my co-author, Andrew Krueger, whose dedication to the subject matter and the making of this book was exceptional.

Our many conversations about the Internet and economic development were a reward of writing this book.

Special thanks are given to my wife, Agnes Briones Ubalde, who endured my late nights and weekends writing—and especially for putting up with me telling my online dating story in this book. Thank you also to my son, Talio, who demanded that I take writing breaks so we could play.

I would also like to thank Jon Roberts and Dean Whittaker, two innovators in economic development who inspire me to keep striving.

Lastly, I want to thank Jeff Finkle and the International Economic Development Council for their commitment to fostering professional development and our partnership in this mission.

Acknowledgements from Andrew Krueger

Firstly, I'd like to thank my co-author, Anatalio Ubalde, for bringing me on board to help write this book. It has been a pleasure to work with Anatalio, and while we both worked very hard to craft this book, it never seemed like work as much as an exciting opportunity to explore and share a subject we are both passionate about. The occasion to produce this book has given me great satisfaction, knowing that it will help make all the communities we call home better places to live, work, and play.

I want to thank my mother, who has supported me unwaveringly and without hesitation through every endeavor I have ever attempted in life (even when it was not to her benefit). Without her, I would be far from where I stand today, struggling to accomplish far simpler achievements.

Finally, I want to thank my father. I know there is no way I would have ever grown up to write about the Internet if he hadn't come home with an IBM 286 or let me use the local university's server room as a giant maze, much to the chagrin of his IT staff.

About the Authors

Anatalio Ubalde, MCP, FM

Anatalio Ubalde is Co-founder and CEO of GIS Planning Inc., an economic development internet company, and ZoomProspector. com, an online site selection and business intelligence service. Mr. Ubalde works with organizations throughout the nation to foster enhanced economic development strategies using Internet technology. His company's strategies are implemented in 42 states and serve the majority of the 100 largest cities in the United States, as well as numerous states and small communities. GIS Planning's ZoomProspector Enterprise web-based GIS product is the industry standard for site selection websites in economic development. In 2007, 2008, 2009, and 2010, GIS Planning made the *Inc.* 5000 list of fastest growing private companies in the United States.

His work in geographic information systems, economic development and the Internet is featured in *The Wall Street Journal, Bloomberg BusinessWeek, Forbes, Fortune, The New York Times, Inc., TechCrunch*, and the U.S. Department of Commerce "Innovative Local Economic Development Programs." In 2009 he was named a Fellow Member of the International Economic Development Council (IEDC) for achieving exceptional stature in the field of economic development. He is also a Board Member of IEDC.

Mr. Ubalde is co-author of the book *Economic Development Marketing: Present & Future*, and author of articles in *Economic Development America, Economic Development Commentary* and the *Canadian Economic Development and Technology Journal*. He is a highly sought-after speaker on the subject of Internet and GIS strategies for effective economic development and has made presentations on these subjects throughout North America, Asia, and Europe.

Before GIS Planning he worked in local economic development with a focus on downtown revitalization, waterfront redevelopment, business attraction/expansion, business retention, and site selection assistance. He has a Master's degree in City Planning from U.C. Berkeley.

Mr. Ubalde is a twenty-four-time United States Master's Diving National Champion, an All-American, and in July of 2010 won two silver medals at the World Masters Championships in Gothenburg, Sweden in springboard and platform diving. He is married to Agnes Briones Ubalde and is the father of Anatalio C. Ubalde, IV.

Andrew Krueger, MCP

Andrew Krueger works as a data analyst with a special interest in data visualization and interactivity. Previously, Mr. Krueger worked as a freelance English teacher in Argentina, a high school English teacher in France, and as a green building consultant for Colliers International in Montenegro and Croatia.

He earned a Bachelor of Arts in Geography and International Studies from the University of Missouri at Columbia, and a Master of City Planning from the University of California at Berkeley. At U.C. Berkeley, he was involved in numerous projects, including land use and pedestrian planning, real estate development, downtown master planning, and policy work in transportation and energy efficiency.

Mr. Krueger caught the travel bug at 17 and hasn't looked back since. He's an avid soccer fan and a lover of languages. In 2014, he plans to be practicing his Portuguese at the World Cup in Brazil.

He lives in Oakland, California.

Why You Paid For This Book When It's Free

You paid for this book mostly because of the expense to physically make and deliver it to you. On the Internet, printing and distribution is free. What you have in your hands is made of atoms, not digital bits.

You can get a free, digital version of the book at: EconomicDevelopmentOnline.com

You may think that giving books away for free is a bad business model because no one makes money from free books. First, the goal of this book isn't to make money; it's to make communities more economically vibrant by leveraging the opportunities of the Internet. If you help a business grow or get someone a better job, you are paying us back in a way that matters more to us than the price of this book. Second, this is a book about sharing information and knowledge through the Internet, and we're practicing what we preach. In this book, we show you how you can be wildly successful if you give information away and are helpful online. So we encourage you to direct your colleagues to get a free copy at this book's website. However, if you feel like you must pay, then we're not going to stop you. But instead of sending us money, please send it to the Diane Lupke Scholarship Fund. It raises funds for the education of economic development professionals working in distressed communities. You can learn more at: http://www.iedconline.org/?p=LupkeFund

Notes

1. In 2007, 2008, 2009 and 2010 GIS Planning Inc. was ranked by Inc. magazine as one of the 5,000 fastest growing private companies in the USA.

2. A term coined by author Seth Godin

3. *The New Rules of Marketing and PR*, by David MeermanScott, 2007, p. xxiv

4. Ibid. p. 11

5. "Web Tools to Put You on the Map," by Katic Burns. "Economic Development Now." 5/13/03. Published by the International Economic Development Council

6. *Economic Development Marketing: Present and Future*, by Anatalio Ubalde, and Eric Simundza. 2008

7. Ibid.

8. http://www.internetworldstats.com

9. United Nations world population estimate: http://www.un.org/esa/population/unpop.htm

10. http://www.guardian.co.uk/business/2009/may/18/digital-content-expansion

11. World Innovation Forum 2010. June 8-9. Nokia Theater, New York

12. http://blogs.hbr.org/now-new-next/2009/05/the-social-data-revolution.html

13. Newsweek, March 19, 2007

14. WEB 3.0 video by Kate Ray: http://vimeo.com/11529540

15. Michigan Technological University, "Web Terms" http://www.mtu.edu/umc/services/web/resources/cms/web.html

16. http://www.pewinternet.org/Infographics/Generational-differences-in-online-activities.aspx

17. Ibid.

18. http://www.pewinternet.org/Static-Pages/Trend-Data/Daily-Internet-Activities-20002009.aspx

19. Nielsen NetRatings 2009

20. In a 2007 conversation I had with Amy Holloway, an Austin-based consultant that used to work in site selection, there are only about 17 boutique site selection companies that focus exclusively on site selection. This does not include corporate real estate professionals that work in real estate development or leasing companies.

21. *Permission marketing: turning strangers into friends, and friends into customers*. New York: Simon & Schuster. 1999

22. *The New Rules of Marketing & PR*. David Meerman Scott. 2010. p. 24

23. *The Future of Public Relations*. Presentation by Lee Rainie. 8/22/2010

24. Several months ago I was talking with Nolan Bushnell, founder of Atari, about strategies for growth and managing innovation. He shared the value of riding the S-curve and provided a conceptual framework for the value proposition new organizations would receive from joining ZoomProspector.com.

25. UC Berkeley, in conjunction with GIS Planning, surveyed over 1,000 economic developers to determine their behavior and perceptions regarding economic development marketing. The results were published in the book *Economic Development Marketing: Present and Future* by Ubalde and Simundza. A follow up survey was performed specifically to see how the

recession had affected both attitudes and budgets. The findings were presented by Anatalio Ubalde in "Budgeting in Crisis" at the International Economic Development Council Leadership Summit in the Woodlands, Texas. February 2, 2010.

26. "Budgeting in Crisis" presented by Anatalio Ubalde at the International Economic Development Council Leadership Summit in the Woodlands, Texas. February 2, 2010. Information is based on a national survey of economic developers.

27. Ibid.

28. "Budgeting in Crisis" presented by Anatalio Ubalde at the International Economic Development Council Leadership Summit in the Woodlands, Texas. February 2, 2010. Information is based on a national survey of economic developers.

29. *Economic Development Marketing: Present and Future*, by Anatalio Ubalde, and Eric Simundza. 2008

30. Ibid.

31. Ubalde, Anatalio and Simundza, Eric. *Site Selection in an Information Era*, 2008

32. Donovan, Dennis, personal interview. July 16, 2008

33. "Surfing the Web Leads Startup Company to Find its Site," by Ken Krizner, *Expansion Management,* November 2005

34. Ibid.

35. Personal Interview with John Bradley, Senior VP of TVA Economic Development. 2005

36. "Severstal to beef up production in 2010." *The Commercial Dispatch.* January 13, 2010. http://www.cdispatch.com/news/article.asp?aid=4415

37. "Surfing the Web Leads Startup Company to Find its Site," by Ken Krizner, *Expansion Management,* November 2005

38. Economic Development Leadership LinkedIn Group in the "Has anyone developed a webinar to site selectors as opposed to face-to-face meetings in an effort to reduce costs, if so how was it received and would anyone be willing to share best practices?"

post by Erin Ealum, Business and Economic Development Director, Anchorage Economic Development Corporation. September 14, 2010.

39. *Economic Development Marketing: Present and Future*, by Anatalio Ubalde, and Eric Simundza. 2008

40. Ibid.

41. "Dell Finds GIS More Than OK," by John W. McCurry. *Site Selection*. May 2005

42. Ibid.

43. 2004 Interview with Brenda Workman, Director of Central City Development, Oklahoma City Chamber of Commerce.

44. 2005 personal interview with Roy Williams, President of the Greater Oklahoma City Chamber of Commerce

45. More specifically I didn't understand why when I was doing my Master's Degree I had access to great data, software, and resources to get my school work done, but when I came to do professional work in local economic development I had poor data, antiquated software and computers, and to get good information I still had to sneak back into my old university library using my expired college ID.

46. "Net Results: Vallejo Hopes Web Site Lures Businesses", by Sheila Muto. *The Wall Street Journal*. June 24, 1998.

47. Pew Research Center's Internet & American Life Project. http://pewInternet.org/Reports/2010/Older-Adults-and-Social-Media/Report/Implications.aspx

48. http://www.facebook.com/press/info.php?statistics; http://www.google.com/adplanner/static/top1000

49. http://weblogs.hitwise.com/heather-dougherty/2010/03/facebook_reaches_top_ranking_i.html

50. Nielsen Wire. http://blog.nielsen.com/nielsenwire/online_mobile/facebook-users-average-7-hrs-a-month-in-january-as-digital-universe-expands

51. http://developers.facebook.com/blog/post/382

52. http://techcrunch.com/2010/05/11/facebook-social-plugins

53. http://developers.facebook.com/blog/post/379

54. http://developers.facebook.com/blog/post/382

55. http://www.allfacebook.com/facebook-tests-show-seo-may-be-possible-with-open-graph-2010-06

56. LinkedIn blog. http://blog.linkedin.com/2009/10/14/linkedin-50-million-professionals-worldwide

57. "Twitter on the Barricades: Six Lessons Learned" by Noam Cohen, *The New York Times*. June 20, 2009. http://www.nytimes.com/2009/06/21/weekinreview/21cohenweb.html?_r=3&hp

58. Twitter Blog. http://blog.twitter.com

59. Personal interview with Ryan Shell, September 17, 2010.

60. http://www.nytimes.com/2010/09/13/technology/13broadband.html

61. http://twitter.com/wired/status/24403888674

62. Morgan Stanley *Mobile Internet Report*. December 2009. http://www.morganstanley.com/institutional/techresearch/mobile_Internet_report122009.html

63. Comscore May 2010 US Online Video Rankings. http://www.comscore.com

64. Comscore May 2010 US Search Engine Rankings. http://www.comscore.com

65. Cisco Visual Networking Index Forecast, 2009-2014. http://www.cisco.com/en/US/netsol/ns827/networking_solutions_sub_solution.html#~forecast

66. http://help.slideshare.com/entries/57394-what-file-formats-does-slideshare-support-what-is-the-maximum-allowed-file-size

67. http://www.slideshare.net/about

68. http://www.syndic8.com

69. "Top 20 Most Popular Blogs, August 2010" eBizMBA, August

2010.

70. http://recruiting.jobvite.com/resources/social-recruiting-survey.php

71. http://techcrunch.com/2010/05/12/facebook-ads-socia-recruiting-tool

72. http://search.twitter.com

73. Data collected from GIS Planning clients in 2010.

74. Radicati Group http://www.radicati.com/?p=3237

75. It used to be the other way around (and for some EDOs it's still this way) in which it was the EDOs working hard to sell the business on why it should locate in its community. However, by empowering people to come to their own conclusions it's a more effective way to convince the business because they feel more confident of their decision because they have control. This is not an insignificant change in the model for empowering the customer to choose your community.

76. United States Small Business Administration. 2007

77. http://www.web2expo.com/webexsf2008/public/schedule/detail/3483

78. The development of this network was something that GIS Planning implemented when we first launched ZoomProspector.com. It aggregated all of our clients' properties into one website that provided national site selection assistance services including demographic, business, and geographic search. After launching the website we developed partnerships with leading corporate real estate site location publications and integrated our ZoomProspector.com website directly into their websites and advertised the service in their publications. This enables our clients to access all of the visibility available through the site selection professionals visiting these other websites.

79. http://www.mattcutts.com/blog/what-google-knows-about-spam

80. http://www.seomoz.org

81. Piper Jaffray, "The New eCommerce Decade: The Age of Micro Targeting." October 2006.

82. *Economic Development Marketing: Present and Future*, 2008 and "Budgeting in Crisis" presented by Anatalio Ubalde at the International Economic Development Council Leadership Summit in the Woodlands, Texas. February 2, 2010. Information is based on a national survey of economic developers.

83. "Budgeting in Crisis" presented by Anatalio Ubalde at the International Economic Development Council Leadership Summit in the Woodlands, Texas. February 2, 2010. Information is based on a national survey of economic developers.

84. *Super Crunchers*: Why Thinking-by-Numbers Is the New Way to Be Smart. Ayers, Ian. 2007

85. http://www.google.com/analytics

86. http://www.google.com/support/analytics/bin/answer. py?hl=en&answer=55591

87. *Web Analytics 2.0.* Avinash Kaushik. 2010

88. http://www.youtube.com/watch?v=o2LJliORQPQ

89. http://www.google.com/websiteoptimizer

90. Experts were located in two ways. First, several thousand were identified in an extensive canvassing of scholarly, government, and business documents from the period 1990-1995 to see who had ventured predictions about the future impact of the Internet. Several hundred of them participated in the first three surveys conducted by Pew Internet and Elon University, and they were re-contacted for this survey. Second, expert participants were hand-picked due to their positions as stakeholders in the development of the Internet.

91. Pew Research Center's Internet & American Life Project. *The future of cloud computing.* http://pewinternet.org/Reports/2010/ The-future-of-cloud-computing/Overview.aspx?r=1

92. Morgan Stanley *Mobile Internet Report.* December 15, 2009. http://www.morganstanley.com/institutional/techresearch/

mobile_internet_report122009.html

93. Cisco Visual Networking Index Forecast, 2009-2014. http://www.cisco.com/en/US/netsol/ns827/networking_solutions_sub_solution.html#~forecast

94. Pew Research Center's Internet & American Life Project. http://pewinternet.org/Reports/2010/Mobile-Access-2010.aspx

95. Morgan Stanley *Mobile Internet Report.* December 15, 2009. http://www.morganstanley.com/institutional/techresearch/mobile_internet_report122009.html

96. http://www.yelp.com/about

97. TechCrunch & August Capital *Social Currency CrunchUp*, July 30, 2010

98. *Crossing the Chasm: Marketing and Selling High-Tech Products to Mainstream Customers,* by Geoffrey A. Moore. Originally published in 1991 and updated in 1999.

99. This concept of very good being average is something I learned from the writings of Seth Godin. I'm paraphrasing much of the logic he lays out in his books for economic development in this section of this book. Based on everything I know about him from his writing and from talking with him personally I know he wants his ideas to spread like viruses and that's exactly what I'm doing here. Now I'm going to go on a tangent, but these are the endnotes anyway, and if you are the type of person that reads endnotes you probably enjoy extra nuggets of information. I met Seth Godin in 2008 and we talked about ZoomProspector.com, which we had just launched a few weeks before. He signed his latest book for me and put the shortest inscription I've ever received in a book. It just shows how well he gets what ZoomProspector.com is and what economic developers do. Here is a picture of us and what he wrote:

Anatalio Ubalde and Seth Godin, Washington D.C., October 2008.

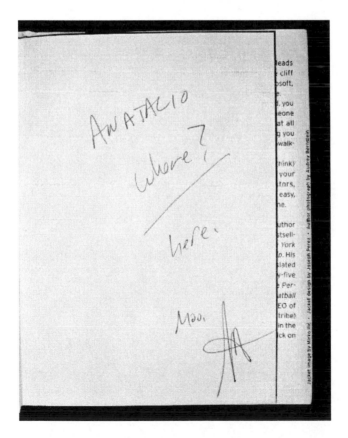